THE PEMBROKE WELSH CORGI

Family Friend and Farmhand

S USAN M. E WING

HOWELL BOOK HOUSE

NEW YORK

Howell Book House
IDG Books Worldwide, Inc.
An International Data Group Company
919 E. Hillsdale Boulevard
Suite 400
Foster City, CA 94404

Library of Congress Cataloging-in-Publication Data:

Ewing, Susan.
The Pembroke Welsh Corgi: family friend and farmhand/Susan Ewing.
        p. cm.
        Includes bibliographical references (p. 173)
        ISBN 1-58245-152-4
        1. Pembroke Welsh corgi. I. Title.

Manufactured in the United States of America
10 9 8 7 6 5 4 3 2 1

2151 8310 5/01

Cover and book design by George J. McKeon

For general information on IDG Books Worldwide's books in the U.S., please call
our Consumer Customer Service department at 800-762-2974. For reseller information, including discounts and premium sales, please call our Reseller Customer
Service department at 800-434-3422.

Acknowledgments

I always thought a dedication to a book would be easy, and, in the case of a book about Corgis, in my fantasy that dedication would be "It's Marsha's Fault," Marsha being Marsha Landon, who got me started with this wonderful breed. Marsha certainly deserves to be mentioned, but I can't leave out my family: my ever patient husband, Jim (who insisted I get a computer table, and a "real" chair), my mother, Joyce Morris (who fed us all summer and even did my ironing), and my brother, Greg, as well as the memory of my father, Robert Morris, and my maternal grandmother, Gladys Taylor, both of whom believed in and supported my desire to write. Also, my "friends of the heart" Larry and Pat Rapple, Janice Anagnost, as well as Walt Strahl, who missed this, but who would have said, "Way to go, Kid!"

Then there are all the people I talked to about Corgis and what they do, and those who willingly shared pictures of their favorite dogs. The performance-events people were especially generous in giving me suggestions of even more people to talk to and beg pictures from. Special thanks to Dr. Lucy Jones, breeder/veterinarian.

The staff at Jamestown Veterinary Hospital answered some strange questions, and enormous thanks go to Drs. William Seleen, Jr. and Sandra Wu of that practice.

To borrow from Don Marquis, thanks to "Babs" Land, "with Babs knows what and Babs knows why." Thanks also to Senior Editor Scott Prentzas for patience and support.

Bottom line, this book never would have happened without Dominique DeVito of Howell Book House. The saying is, "It takes a whole village to raise a child." It's the same with a book. It's not an isolated process, and I thank everyone who encouraged and supported me.

Contents

Introduction

There's an old vaudeville joke in which the comic says, "I got a lot of advice on my act, but I decided to do it anyway." I feel that way about this book. I got a lot of feedback that there was already a book on Pembroke Welsh Corgis, but I decided to write this one anyway.

There is an excellent book on Corgis, *The New Complete Pembroke Welsh Corgi*, by Deborah Harper, and it's packed with terrific information, but I wanted this book to be lighter. I wanted it to be a guide for first-time owners who weren't sure what they wanted to try with their Corgi. Conformation? Obedience? Herding? Therapy? Couch potato? I wanted to present the options and suggest new ideas. Most of all, I wanted Corgi owners, old and new, to have fun. Old timers: Do you remember your first time in the ring? Did you always know what a major was? Was your very first dog a champion, or was there trial and error? And when was the last time you did something new and different with your Corgi? If you've always shown in conformation, try obedience or agility. Newcomers: Have your read the standard? Did you get your dog from a reputable breeder who will be there for you when you have questions? Do you dream of Westminster? Do you have a herd of cows to move?

Corgis have changed physically over the years, but they are still wonderful, smart, active, loving companions, and we owe it to them, and to us, to enjoy what they offer. This book is an attempt to introduce, or reintroduce, readers to that joy.

"They wanted a useful dog . . . they wanted a Corgi." Ch. Evanwhit's On the Other Hand, CD, PT (Marvin), shows that Corgis are versatile. Owners: Karen and Alex Martinac. (Photo by Linda Leeman/EWE-TOPIA)

CHAPTER 1

A Profile of the Pembroke Welsh Corgi— Is It Right for You?

Pembroke Welsh Corgis have been around for hundreds of years, and over that time they have evolved into intelligent, sturdy, independent and bold dogs.

Farmers of the Welsh hills wanted a dog that was an "easy keeper," one that wouldn't eat them out of house and home. They wanted a guard dog as well as a family pet for the children. They also wanted a useful dog, a dog that would drive the cattle or geese to market and maybe even retrieve game. And they wanted a dog with a "wash-and-wear" coat that would easily shed the mud of the fields without a lot of fussy grooming. In short, they wanted a Corgi.

A Working Dog's Coat

Study the old photographs of the early Corgis and compare those dogs with today's Corgi. You'll see that although there have been changes over the years, the basics are still there. The Corgi is still a compact, sturdy dog that makes both a diligent worker and a dedicated family dog.

Because Corgis are herding dogs, they have been bred to be independent thinkers as well as quick, busy and active dogs. These dogs are not for everyone, although most Corgi owners think there is no other breed!

The Corgi has what is called a "double coat," meaning that a softer, finer coat lies under its harsher, heavier outer coat. This outer coat protects the dog from the elements, while the undercoat provides warmth and dryness. For an illustration of this, pour water over a Corgi's back and then part the fur to the skin. Chances are, the skin is completely dry. The coat's medium length also prevents dirt and burrs from clinging, and any dirt that does stick can be brushed away easily. The coat doesn't mat or tangle, either, which can be a real plus in a family pet.

The negative side to this coat is that Corgis *do* shed. Regular grooming will keep the hair under control, but be prepared for heavy shedding twice a year and a milder hair loss all the time. Corgis don't need professional grooming care, but they do need regular brushing to control the loss of undercoat.

A Dog for Small Quarters

Corgis don't take up much space, so they fit well into apartment life, as long as they are provided with long outdoor walks or some other physical activity. These are moderately high-energy dogs—they're not hyper, but they do need exercise. After all, Corgis were bred to work. Fortunately, because of their size, an active game of fetch played indoors can help give them the exercise they need.

Despite the breed's weather-resistant coat, Corgis are not meant to live outdoors or in a kennel. Even more important, they are eager and willing to please, and they like to be with their people. If you don't have the time or inclination to allow your Corgi to share your house, get another breed.

Ch. Evanwhit's On the Other Hand, CD, PT, takes a break from keeping the sheep in line. Owners: Karen and Alex Martinac. (Photo by Linda Leeman/EWE-TOPIA)

THE CORGI TEMPERAMENT

The Corgi looks like a small dog, but it's more appropriate to think of it as a short-legged big dog—more like a German Shepherd Dog with short legs than a toy lap dog.

Corgis are indeed short, but the trouble is, they don't know that. Inside, they are *big*. They are fearless in the face of almost any obstacle. This is not good when the obstacle is an Irish Wolfhound that your male Corgi is inviting to "step outside." Neither is it good when you have your dog on a grooming table and he decides that he'd rather be on the ground. Sometimes you have to provide Corgis with the caution they seem to lack.

Because they are big dogs with short legs, Corgis can take the rough and tumble of play with children, without much fear of harming themselves. A properly conditioned Corgi can go for long hikes with the family, although the short legs do make it a bit harder for a Corgi to keep up with a jogger or a biker. Corgis generally enjoy water, too, although, again, their short legs may make it hard for them to get out of a pool. If you have a pool, supervise the dog carefully.

Corgis take well to training of all kinds, although their quick intelligence is not always a plus. They learn quickly—although whether they will actually do what they've learned can be another story! Some Corgis like to add their own interpretation to the lesson learned; others need

Corgis take well to training of all kinds. Ch. Fours Bust-A-Buns Tuf E. Nuf, HS (Tuffy), practices his jumping for agility. Owners: Carol Kelly and Charles Kruger. (Photo by Linda Leeman/EWE-TOPIA)

more motivation than just pleasing their owner. Some Corgis seem to wonder, Why should I leave this comfortable spot just because you are calling?

The Corgi and Children

A Corgi that is raised with children is almost always good with them. Corgis can take the rough-and-tumble of playing with children, and most will retrieve a tennis ball for as long as you keep throwing it. There are no children in our household, though, so I try to take our young dogs to places where there are children. This seems to have worked as well, and they get along with children nicely. Small children frequently pet our dogs

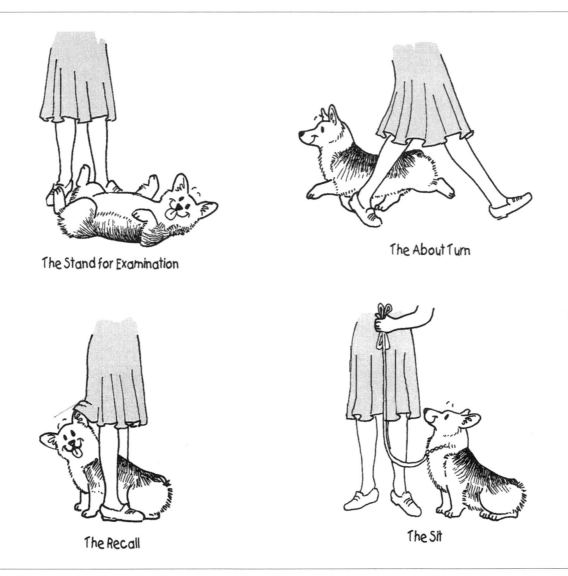

The Stand for Examination

The About Turn

The Recall

The Sit

Corgis like to add their own interpretation to the lesson learned. (Drawing by Pat Rapple/Funny Bones)

A Corgi that is raised with children is almost always good to them, as are Llanelly Corgis with Olivia Powers. (Photo by Lucy E. Jones, DVM)

on walks, with no ill effects on either side. Still, because the dogs are not around kids on a regular basis, I try to instruct the youngsters to approach quietly.

Keep in mind that because Corgis are herding dogs, they might want to "herd" members of the group by nudging, pushing, bumping, or gently nipping at heels. So, children running through the yard may find the Corgi at their heels. You can correct this behavior, but realize that it's a lot like stopping a terrier from digging or a sight hound

from running—it's part of the Corgi's genetic makeup to chase and nip. Yes, correct it, but also make your children and their friends aware of the dog's instinctive behavior. Make them understand that the Corgi is not biting or attacking. It is not a vicious dog—it is just herding.

The Corgi and Other Animals

Corgis seem to get along well with other pets in a household as well. Our Corgis do not have a cat as a housemate, but although they are curious about cats, they do not seem to want to chase or hurt them. We used to take our Corgi, Megan, to visit friends who also had a Corgi and a cat. Megan thought that the cat was very interesting and great fun to try to play with. At a bed-and-breakfast once, another of our Corgis, Trilby, encountered two cats. One greeted her face to face and seemed to be telling her that this was a cat's house and that she was a tolerated guest. Trilby made no move to chase or attack that cat. The second cat, however, took one look and fled headlong, with a delighted Trilby chasing after. It was a wonderful game!

Certainly, use caution introducing animals to each other, but, generally speaking, Corgis do fine with cats. They do well with other dogs, too—but again, use caution at the beginning.

Initially, Corgis are less intimidated by smaller dogs. They seem to recognize other Corgis and love to say hello. My dogs have all liked Whippets, and they play well with Schipperkes. They are a little more reserved with larger dogs until they really get to know them.

Keep your dog's vaccinations current, protect against heartworm, check regularly for fleas and ticks, test twice a year for internal parasites, feed good quality dog food, don't let the dog run loose, and you should have a happy, healthy companion for many years. (Photo by Gail Painter)

The Corgi and Its Owner

Corgis are sociable dogs. They do not fawn and cling, but they do like to be with their people, wherever they may be. Both our males had to know exactly where everyone was and what they were doing. Both were worriers who had taken the care of the household upon themselves. Our females have always seemed to be more laid-back and more willing to let us run things without feeling they knew best.

Corgis like to be with their people, wherever that may be. A Valley Vixen Corgi enjoys a boat ride. (Photo by Irma Hilts)

These dogs love to sleep on the sofa or in your chair, but if that's not allowed, they are perfectly willing to curl up in their crate or on a dog bed or an old blanket that you have provided for them. About a year ago, I also would have said that most Corgis will share a couch or chair but don't care about actually being on your lap. However, now we have Hayley, and she thinks that my lap is the very best place to be, especially when the weather is 85° and humid, for some reason! I only hope that she is this affectionate when the temperature drops to 0°.

Corgis definitely like to be part of the action. Most of them love to play with balls or Frisbees. Brecon, our first male, would play forever—he was almost obsessive about chasing and bringing back whatever was thrown. Megan would happily retrieve a tennis ball until I had to stop for her own good. Their daughter, Trilby, had her own version of "fetch," which consisted of sitting and looking very alert and interested while watching the ball soar through the air until it landed. Then she would watch me walk to the ball and retrieve

it. She found it a very interesting form of exercise—for me.

Interestingly, Corgis also like to be the boss—maybe they feel that if they can make big cows obey, a few humans should be easy. They definitely will take a mile if given an inch, so when your enchanting young puppy does something cute and charming, think about whether you will find that same behavior cute and charming when an adult dog does it. If not, don't let it continue! If your decision is to allow the dog on the furniture, fine. But if not, don't start! It's much easier to not start something than it is to stop it.

Remember that Corgis also have somewhat strong wills, so obedience classes should be on your list of things to do with your dog. You don't have to train your dog to advanced levels or enter

If your decision is to allow the dog on the furniture, fine. But if not, don't start! (Photo by Winter/Churchill)

Obedience competitions (although it's a wonderful activity) to benefit from classes. But you do need to let your Corgi know, firmly and gently, that *you* are the boss. Praise and food rewards go a long way with a Corgi, and most dogs seem to enjoy training sessions.

YOUR FIRST CORGI

Fortunately, Corgis housetrain very easily and quickly. Use a crate, and you (and your home) may survive the early weeks with only one or two accidents. (For more on the wonders of crate training, see Chapter 5, "Living with Your Pembroke Welsh Corgi.")

Corgis are not terribly destructive as puppies, but they *are* puppies. For about the first year, especially during teething, they will definitely chew. They love to explore because they're full of

curiosity. With our male puppy, Griffin, this meant tipping over every wastebasket he could reach and shredding and tearing whatever was in it. I gave up putting anything in my office wastebasket for a year, and even at that age, he still loves to tip over the basket and chew on the edge. He doesn't touch the contents anymore—I think he just does it to keep me alert. Mild-mannered Hayley, however, never chewed anything except a pair of my husband's shoes. By the time Corgis are a year old, most things should be safe, but it doesn't hurt to monitor the dogs just the same. Our Heather stole and chewed pencils all her life, and she once ate an entire bowl of cashews. (This didn't bother her a bit, but it definitely ruined the cocktail hour.)

Corgis are full of curiosity. A Cymry pup checks out the contents of a cup. (Photo by Kathryn Smith)

On the whole, Corgis are healthy dogs as well. The breed has very little incidence of hip dysplasia, and von Willebrand's disease, a blood disorder that has affected the breed, seems to be much less frequent. It's still a good idea to make sure that your dog's parents have been tested for any eye anomalies and for von Willebrand's disease, but otherwise, there are not many major health concerns. Corgis have a life expectancy of about 14 years, although Corgis living to age 16 or 17 are not unheard of.

As an owner, however, you've got some responsibilities, which will be covered in later chapters: Keep your dog's vaccinations current, protect against heartworm, check regularly for fleas and ticks, test once or twice a year for internal parasites, feed good-quality dog food, and don't let the dog run loose. You should have a happy, healthy companion for many years.

Whatever their origin, the Corgi has helped humans at work for centuries. Joe Kapelos with Marvin (Ch. Evanwhit's On the Other Hand, CD, PT). Owners: Karen and Alex Martinac. (Photo by Linda Leeman/EWE-TOPIA)

CHAPTER 2

A Brief History of the Pembroke Welsh Corgi

To explore the origins of the Pembroke Welsh Corgi, let's first take a look at the definition of the word *Corgi*.

The *Oxford English Dictionary* (second edition) notes that the word *Corgi* has its roots in the Welsh words for *dwarf* and *dog* and offers the following definition: "Corgi Also Corgy. Pl corgis, corgwn. A short-legged dog of Welsh origin, with a head resembling that of a fox." It goes on to cite references of the earliest instances of the word appearing in print. A characteristic one is this excerpt that appeared in *Observer* in 1930: "What can one say of the Welsh Corgis . . . with their truncated legs, prick ears, foxy heads, and longish bodies?" Another descriptive reference appeared in a 1934 *Punch* article: "It had a face like a fox and ears that stood up like a fox's . . . . its body was short and stocky, and it had no tail at all; nothing but half-an-inch of stump. 'And what kind of mongrel is this?' I asked. 'Mongrel!' she exclaimed. 'It's no mongrel; it's the latest thing in pets. It's a Corgi.'"

Every reference book that mentions Cardigan and Pembroke Welsh Corgis acknowledges the greater age of the Cardigan breed, while still giving the Pembroke Welsh Corgi its due as a relatively old breed. From there, things tend to branch off into whatever theory the author favors.

THEORIES OF THE CORGI'S ROOTS

The most complete histories are found in *The Complete Pembroke Welsh Corgi,* by Mary Gay Sargent and Deborah S. Harper, and in *The New Complete Pembroke Welsh Corgi,* by Deborah S. Harper. The latter covers three separate theories that, taken together, present a very plausible history of the Pembroke Welsh Corgi.

The first theory, that the two breeds had entirely separate origins, is held by W. Lloyd-Thomas, writing in an article that appeared in *American Kennel Club Gazette* in 1935:

> *The Pembroke and Cardigan Welsh Corgis originated as two entirely separate and unrelated breeds, the Pembroke being a member of the large Spitz family and the Cardigan evolving from the Dachshund or Tekel class. Members of the Spitz family, such as the Schipperke, the Pomeranian, the Keeshond, and the Samoyed, are characterized by prick ears, a pointed muzzle, and (in most) a curly tail. The Tekel group, which includes the Dachshund and the Basset Hound, are essentially long-bodied, deep-chested, short-legged dogs, heavier in muzzle than typical Spitz types.*

According to the Harper book, Lloyd-Thomas maintained that the Cardigan breed influenced the breed that was to become the Pembroke, "but that the traffic in puppies never flowed the other way." Lloyd-Thomas also states that changes in the original Cardigan were the result of intermixing with other breeds, but not with the Pembroke:

> *The Cardigan Corgi's gradual refinement and somewhat diminished size from that of the original Corgi, along with a change of ear carriage from a drooping ear to an erect, slightly hooded ear, plus changes in coat quality, all supposedly were brought about by the influence of breeds other than the Pembroke Corgi . . .*

What I find interesting about this quote is the reference to Cardigan Corgis having drooping ears. If you take a Cardigan's ears and hold them down to simulate a drop ear, you can easily see that they are not Spitz-descended, but that they indeed have a heavier, more hound-like head.

Another theory explained in *The New Complete Pembroke Welsh Corgi* is that of Clifford Hubbard. He starts with the premise that there was one original Welsh Corgi herding dog and that Viking invasions introduced the Swedish cattle dog, the Vallhund or Vastergotland Spitz. The Vallhund, which is very similar to the Pembroke Welsh Corgi, was crossed with the native herd dog.

> *Two distinctly different Corgi types began to develop; the original short-legged, long-bodied, deep-chested dog with droopy ears remained as the Cardiganshire Corgi, while the Corgi of the Pembrokeshire region took on many of the Spitz-like characteristics of the Vallhund.*

Hubbard further postulated that the Spitz characteristics seen in the Pembroke Corgi as a result of the Vallhund influence were subsequently accentuated by crosses with dogs thought to be either Schipperkes or early Pomeranians. These came to South Wales with Flemish weavers when they settled in Pembrokeshire in about A.D. 1107.

Whether from Vallhunds, Lancaster Heelers or Flemish imports, Corgis have inherited an instinct to herd. Desperado's Young Gun, PT, CD. (Photo by Linda Leeman/EWE-TOPIA)

Swedish Vallhund bitch, Litton of Duncliffe of Ormareon, a winner in the English show ring, shows the similarity to the Pembroke Welsh Corgi. The Vallhund can have a natural bobtail. (Photo by Gail Smyka)

Modern Vallhund tail sets also reinforce the theory that there is a connection between Vallhunds and Pembroke Welsh Corgis. Vallhunds may be born with a naturally short, or bob, tail, as is also the case with Pembrokes. Or, their tail may curl over their back in typical Spitz fashion. Pictures of Pembroke Welsh Corgis with natural tails frequently show those tails as curling over the back.

To see a Vallhund does make this theory seem very believable, but the question of color crops up, as does the existence of another short little dog with erect ears, the Lancashire Heeler. The Vallhund is typically wolf-gray, a color found in other Spitz breeds such as the Keeshond and the Norwegian Elkhound, but not the Corgi. While claiming that the dominant red or sable colors of the Flemish dogs obliterated the Vallhund coloring in the Pembroke Corgi, Hubbard overlooked a matter of color when he used the Lancashire Heeler as another example of a Spitz-like heeling dog that he considered closely related to the Swedish Vallhund:

The Lancashire Heeler, a small black and tan cattle dog quite similar in appearance to the Corgi, has existed for centuries in northern England. . . . The late Miss Eve Forsyth-Forrest . . . believed the existence of the Lancashire Heeler substantiated her theory that the Corgi was the original native dog of Britain. Accordingly, at the time of the Saxon invasions, some Britons fled into the depths of the Forest of Elmet, and it was there a pocket of their Corgi-like Lancashire Heelers survived the passing centuries. The suggestion that the early Corgis, both Pembroke and Cardigan, were commonly black and tan in color strengthens the theory of a probable link between the Corgi breeds and the Lancashire Heeler. The pronounced similarity in appearance, as well as in the instinctive guarding and herding capabilities shared by the Pembroke Corgi and the Swedish Vallhund, leaves little doubt that their paths have crossed. Just when and where will most likely remain another matter of conjecture.

The third theory, discussed in Harper's book and presented in 1987 by Iris Combe, is my favorite because it ties the Pembroke Corgi to a breed I find fascinating, the Lundehund. The Lundehund was used to hunt puffins and, to that end, has extra toes for gripping the rocks, has prick ears, and is double-jointed to enable the dog to enter and leave puffin burrows easily. These dogs also are red and white, with light sable markings. Combe, working with Nordic canine researchers, points out that the trade in feathers, meat, and oils from various seabirds became important to the Scandinavian economy.

In the eighth century, Vikings were known to have made annual spring trips to the British off-shore islands as far south as Anglesey in northern Wales in search of these valuable commodities. Presumably the travelers brought with them dogs that had proven themselves to be useful in this endeavor.

COMMON GROUND

All these theories have points in their favor, and when you explore some of the breeds mentioned in them, you can find other pieces of common ground—or at least common belief.

In *The Atlas of Dog Breeds of the World*, by Bonnie Wilcox, DVM, and Chris Walkowicz, some interesting points are found. Cardigan Corgi origins are traced to 1200 B.C., and Pembrokes are traced to the tenth century, with reference to both Flemish weavers and to Swedish Vallhunds. The Lundehund is believed to be a very old breed. It stands between 12½ inches and 14½ inches, and weighs about 14 pounds. The Swedish Vallhund weighs between 20 and 32 pounds, stands between 13 and 16 inches, and has a natural bobtail, a feature that does occasionally show up in Pembroke Corgi litters. Although the preferred color is shaded gray, shaded red (with or without white) is allowed.

Sinbad of Wey, TDX, UD, CDX, with owner Kenneth Butler. Although Corgis are not commonly seen in the fields today, it is probable that as all-around dogs in the early days in Wales, they were sporting dogs as much as working or herding dogs. As late as 1959, an AKC Gazette column recommends the Corgi for its ability to "trail, locate, and recover" game in the field.

Schipperke-like dogs are mentioned as likely ancestors of the Pembroke in *Dogs: Breeds, Care, and Training*, by Shirlee A. Kalstone. The 1997 edition of *The Complete Dog Book*, compiled by the American Kennel Club, states, "An early progenitor of the Pembroke Welsh Corgi of today has been described as having a noticeable resemblance to the old Schipperkes." It further speaks of Spitz characteristics with "little or no Dachshund characteristics." Under the listing for the Cardigan Corgi is, "The dog is a member of the same family that has produced the Dachshund."

Dickie Albin refers to a Pembroke's possible Spitz ancestry and Dachshund ancestery behind the Cardigan in her book *The Family Welsh Corgi.*

It is obvious that there is a real mix in the background of the Pembroke Welsh Corgi. Study of the modern Vallhund makes a connection there seem positive, and other crosses could easily have introduced the variety of colors and patterns seen in the modern Pembroke. Students of the breed can, no doubt, argue reasonably for or against any of the possibilities of ancestry, from Lundehunds to Schipperkes.

Leslie Perrins, author of *The Welsh Corgi,* doesn't see any point in worrying about the ancestry much at all. Perrins says that most owners want only a brief summary, and that is what he gives them: "There was some infusion of the ancestors of the Buhund, the Vallund and the Finnehund, and this cross may have been to some extent responsible for the Corgi's head as we know it today."

The author who perhaps captures best the commonsense side of the argument of what made the Corgi what it is today was Charles Lister-Kaye, in his book *The Popular Welsh Corgi:*

> *The origin and early history of the Welsh Corgi is lost in the mists of time; the only thing we can be sure of is that Corgis have existed in southwest Wales for some hundreds of years. It is a common failing among doggy writers to attempt to ascribe breed origins to members of the canine race depicted in drawings on Egyptian tombs. But such efforts are not impressive, for, whatever breed one selects, long or short, prick- or drop-eared, leggy or otherwise, a delineation will be found in some tomb or other which can be seized upon and claimed as the "father and mother" of the breed under review. . . . Surely it is better to admit that we know nothing of the Corgi as, and if, it existed a thousand years ago and more? If we can get back a few hundreds we are doing pretty well. . . . We do at least know that both breeds have occupied a very special place in the pastoral economy of the Welsh counties with which they have had a long and honourable association.*

Of course, all the theories in the world mean absolutely nothing if you have given your heart to a Corgi. With their bright eyes, quick intelligence, beautiful coats and perfect size, who cares? It's fun to study the theories regarding the breed's origin, but my favorite explanation is in this poem, "Corgi Fantasy," by Anne G. Biddlecome, used here with permission of The Welsh Corgi League.

> *Would you know where Corgis came from?*
> *How they came to live with mortals?*
>
> *Hearken to the ancient legend,*
> *Hearken to the story-teller.*
>
> *On the mountains of the Welsh-land*
> *In its green and pleasant valleys,*
> *Lived the peasant folk of old times,*
> *Lived our fathers and grandfathers;*
> *And they toiled and laboured greatly*
> *With their cattle and their ploughing,*
> *That their women might have plenty,*
> *And their children journeyed daily*

With the kine upon the mountain,
Seeing that they did not wander,
Did not come to any mischief,
While their fathers ploughed the valley
And their mothers made the cheeses.

'Til one day they found two puppies
Found them playing in a hollow,
Playing like a pair of fox-cubs.
Burnished gold their coat and colour,
Shining like a piece of satin—
Short and straight and thick their forelegs
And their heads were like a fox's.

But their eyes were kind and gentle;
Long of body were these dwarf dogs
And without a tail behind them.

Now the children stayed all day there,
And they learned to love the dwarf-dogs,
Shared their bread and water with them,
Took them home with them at even.
Made a cosy basket for them,
Made them welcome in the kitchen
Made them welcome in the homestead.

When the men came home at sunset
Saw them lying in the basket,
Heard the tale the children told them,
How they found them on the mountain
Found them playing in the hollow—
They were filled with joy and wonder
Said it was a fairy present,
Was a present from the wee folk,
For their fathers told a legend
How the fairies kept some dwarf dogs.

Called them Corgis—Fairy heelers:
Made them work the fairy cattle,
Made them pull the fairy coaches,
Made them steeds for fairy riders,
Made them fairy children's playmates;
Kept them hidden in the mountains,
Kept them in the mountains' shadow
Lest the eye of mortal see one.

Now the Corgis grew and prospered,
And the fairies' life was in them,
In the lightness of their movement,
In the quickness of their turning,
In their badness and their goodness.
And they learnt to work for mortals,
Learnt to love their mortal masters
Learnt to work their masters' cattle,
Learnt to play with mortal children.

Now in every vale and hamlet,
In the valleys and the mountains,
From the little town of Tenby,
By the Port of Milford Haven,
To St. David's Head and Fishguard,
In the valley of the Cleddau,
On the mountains of Preselly,
Lives the Pembrokeshire Welsh Corgi,
Lives the Corgi with his master.

Should you doubt this ancient story,
Laugh and scoff and call it nonsense,
Look and see the saddle markings
Where the fairy warriors rode them
(As they ride them still at midnight,
On Midsummer's Eve at midnight,
When we mortals all are sleeping.)

THE CORGI'S RECENT HISTORY

More recent history is much easier to follow, both in Great Britain and in the United States. While there is a record of show classes being offered by the Bancyfelin Horticultural and Agricultural Society in 1892, it was not until 1925 that the first Corgi classes were held under Kennel Club rules. Pembrokes and Cardigans were judged together because the Kennel Club did not acknowledge them as two separate breeds until 1934.

Popularity in England was helped along when King George VI decided to buy a Corgi puppy for his daughter, Princess Elizabeth. Rozavel Golden Eagle, later called "Dookie," became the first in a long line of Pembroke Welsh Corgis owned by the royal family.

Corgis descended from "Dookie" are still to be found at Buckingham Palace, and Corgis are also a part of the household at Clarence House, residence of the Queen Mother. Members of the royal family frequently attend Corgi judging at Crufts and a the shows at Windsor.

In 1933, Mrs. Lewis Roesler fell in love with a Pembroke Welsh Corgi and brought her from England to her home in Massachusetts. Little Madam became the first Pembroke Welsh Corgi registered with the American Kennel Club and was registered as a Welsh Corgi. However, by 1935,

Eng. Ch. Crymmych President (Newman Chatter ex Crymmych Beauty), whelped in 1929, sired 11 English champions, including C Rozavel Red Dragon.

Eng. Ch. Rozavel Red Dragon (Eng. Ch. Crymmych President ex Felcourt Flame), whelped in 1932, exerted a profound influence on the breed, passing on type, stamina, intelligence and personality.

Eng./Can./Am. Ch. Bowhit Pivot (Eng. Ch. Crymmych President ex Chalcot Saucebox), whelped in 1933, was the first American Pembroke Champion.

Ch. Little Madam of Merriedip, a Bowhit Pepper daughter, was the first Pembroke Welsh Corgi to be registered with the American Kennel Club in 1934.

the two separate breeds were acknowledged with the registration of Cardigan Welsh Corgi Blodwen of Robinscroft. In 1936, The Pembroke Welsh Corgi Club of America was founded and held its first specialty show in conjunction with the Morris and Essex show. The total number of Pembroke Welsh Corgis registered at that time was 33, and the Morris and Essex shows drew seven Pembroke entries. Of those seven, three were sired by Ch.

Bowhit Pivot, and two by Bowhit Pepper. As a point of comparison, in 1998, the American Kennel Club registered 8,932 Pembroke Welsh Corgis, and the national specialty show drew an entry of 362.

Clearly, Corgis have grown immensely in popularity. After all, who wouldn't love these dogs?

CHAPTER 3

Official Standard of the Pembroke Welsh Corgi

The breed standard for the Pembroke Welsh Corgi is the written guideline that describes the breed and tells you that a dog is a Corgi. It is designed to help breeders and judges determine the best of the breed, and it is based on the history of the breed and on what the dog was bred to do. The Pembroke Welsh Corgi standard is one of the most comprehensive standards—not only is it very clear on what is required, but in most cases, it also explains why.

The Pembroke Welsh Corgi Club of America is working on a new illustrated standard using actual photographs instead of line drawings, and this will be quite helpful. Also useful and a worthwhile investment is the AKC video of the standard, which gives the viewer a chance to see the Corgi in motion and to study good and bad points on a real dog. Read the standard, study the pictures, attend some dog shows and learn and enjoy!

The following is the official standard for the Pembroke Welsh Corgi as approved by the Pembroke Welsh Corgi Club of America. My notes regarding various points of this standard will appear in italics.

A correct Corgi is low-set, strong and sturdily built. (Photo by Gail Painter)

BODY TYPE

GENERAL APPEARANCE Low-set, strong, sturdily built and active, giving an impression of substance and stamina in a small space. Should not be so low and heavy-boned as to appear coarse or overdone, nor so light-boned as to appear racy. Outlook bold, but kindly. Expression intelligent and interested. Never shy or vicious.

Correct type, including general balance and outline, attractiveness of headpiece, intelligent outlook, and correct temperament is of primary importance. Movement is especially important, particularly as viewed from the side. A dog with a smooth and free gait has to be reasonably sound and must be highly regarded. A minor fault must never take precedence over the above desired qualities.

A dog must be very seriously penalized for the following faults, regardless of whatever desirable qualities the dog may present: oversized or undersized; button, rose, or drop ears; overshot or undershot bite; fluffies, whitelies, mismarks, or bluies.

A Corgi was bred to work, and this is reflected in the standard's attention to balance and movement. A certain level of quickness and flexibility in a Corgi enables it to herd. Furthermore, a dog that is out of balance and that does not move freely will tire quickly. The side gait of a Corgi should be smooth and the topline level. The front legs should have adequate reach, and the rear legs should have adequate extension. A short, choppy gait wastes energy in an up-and-down motion and quickly tires the dog.

SIZE, PROPORTION, SUBSTANCE Height (from ground to highest point on withers) should be 10 to 12 inches. Weight is in proportion to size, not exceeding 30 pounds for dogs and 28 pounds for bitches. In show condition, the preferred medium-sized dog of correct bone and substance will weigh approximately 27 pounds, with bitches approximately 25 pounds. Obvious oversized specimens and diminutive toy-like individuals must be very severely penalized.

Proportions—Moderately long and low. The distance from the withers to the base of the tail should be approximately 40 percent greater than the

Although this dog has an incorrect coat type, no one can say that this sable fluffy puppy isn't cute! (Photo by Maxine Ellis)

between the ears. Moderate amount of stop. Very slight rounding of cheek, not filled in below the eyes, as the foreface should be nicely chiseled to give a somewhat tapered muzzle. The distance from the occiput to the center of the stop should be greater than the distance from the stop to the nose tip, the proportion being five parts of total distance for the skull and three parts for the foreface. The muzzle should be neither dish-faced nor Roman-nosed. **Eyes**—Oval, medium in size, not round, nor protruding, nor deep-set and pig-like. Set somewhat obliquely. Variations in brown in harmony with coat color. Eye rims dark, preferably black. While dark eyes enhance the expression, true black eyes are most undesirable, as are yellow or bluish eyes. **Ears**—Erect, firm and of medium size, tapering slightly to a rounded point. Ears are mobile, and react sensitively to sounds. A line drawn from the nose tip through the eyes to the ear tips, and across, should form an approximate equilateral triangle. Bat ears, small

distance from the withers to the ground.
Substance—Should not be so low and heavy-boned as to appear coarse or overdone, nor so light-boned as to appear racy.

A Corgi is short, but it cannot be heavy and dragging, nor too lightweight, if it is to do its job correctly. If the dog is too low to the ground, it will not be able to get its legs properly under it for the speed and flexibility required for herding. If it's too tall, its head will not be in the position to nip cow heels—or to duck a kick.

HEAD The head should be foxy in shape and appearance. **Expression**—Intelligent and interested, but not sly. **Skull**—Should be fairly wide and flat

Dark eye rims enhance the expression of this Corgi. (Photo by Gail Painter)

catlike ears, overly large and weak ears, hooded ears, or ears carried too high or too low all are undesirable. Button, rose, or drop ears are very serious faults. **Nose**—Black and fully pigmented. **Mouth**—Scissors bite, the inner side of the upper incisors touching the outer side of the lower incisors. Level bite is acceptable. Overshot or undershot bite is a very serious fault. **Lips**—Black, tight, with little or no fullness.

The proportions of the Corgi head give it an intelligent expression and the classic "foxy" look. The muzzle should be very clean, and the tight lips should have no hint of "flews." The Corgi is not a dog prone to drooling.

NECK, TOPLINE, BODY   **Neck**—Fairly long. Of sufficient length to provide over-all balance of the dog. Slightly arched, clean, and blending well into the shoulders. A very short neck giving a stuffy appearance and a long, thin, or ewe-neck are faulty. **Topline**—Firm and level, neither riding up to nor falling away at the croup. A slight depression behind the shoulders caused by a heavier neck coat meeting the shorter body coat is permissible. **Body**—Rib cage should be well sprung, slightly egg-shaped, and moderately long. Deep chest, well let down between the forelegs. Exaggerated lowness interferes with the desired freedom of movement and should be penalized. Viewed from above, the body should taper slightly to the end of the loin. Loin short. Round or flat rib cage, lack of brisket, extreme length, or cobbiness are undesirable. **Tail**—Docked as short as possible without being indented. Occasionally a puppy is born with a natural dock, which, if sufficiently short, is acceptable. A tail up to 2 inches in length is allowed, but if carried high tends to spoil the contour of the topline.

Correct neck length balances the body and contributes to the dog's smooth, even movement. The dog's deep chest allows for plenty of lung space. The tail is traditionally docked and gives a smooth, finished look to the dog.

FOREQUARTERS   **Legs**—Short, forearms turned slightly inward, with the distance between wrists less than between the shoulder joints, so that the front does not appear absolutely straight. Ample bone carried right down into the feet. Pasterns firm and nearly straight when viewed from the side. Weak pasterns and knuckling over are serious faults. Shoulder blades long and well laid back along the rib cage. Upper arms nearly equal in length to shoulder blades. Elbows parallel to the body, not prominent, and well set back to allow a line perpendicular to the ground to be drawn from the tip of the shoulder blade through to the elbow. **Feet**—Oval, with the two center toes slightly in advance of the two outer ones. Turning neither in nor out. Pads strong and feet arched. Nails short. Dew claws on both forelegs and hind legs usually removed. Too round, long and narrow, or splayed feet are faulty.

HINDQUARTERS   Ample bone, strong and flexible, moderately angulated at stifle and hock. Exaggerated angulation is as faulty as too little. Thighs should be well muscled. Hocks short, parallel, and when viewed from the side are perpendicular to the ground. Barrel hocks or cowhocks are most objectionable. Slipped or double-jointed hocks are very faulty. **Feet**—As in front.

The emphasis on bone and muscle and angulation reinforces the fact that the Corgi is a working dog. Proper structure is necessary for the execution of whatever job the Corgi is given.

COAT AND COLOR

COAT Medium-length, short, thick, weather-resistant undercoat with a coarser, longer outer coat. Overall length varies, with slightly thicker and longer ruff around the neck and chest and on the shoulders. The body coat lies flat. Hair is slightly longer on back of forelegs and underpart, and somewhat fuller and longer on rear of hindquarters. The coat is preferably straight, but some waviness is permitted. This breed has a shedding coat, and seasonal lack of undercoat should not be too severely penalized, providing that the hair is glossy, healthy, and well groomed. A wiry, tightly marcelled coat is very faulty, as is an overly short, smooth, and thin coat. Very serious fault: Fluffies—a coat of extreme length with exaggerated feathering on ears, chest, legs, and feet, underparts, and hindquarters. Trimming such a coat does not make it any more acceptable. The Corgi should be shown in its natural condition, with no trimming permitted except to tidy the feet and, if desired, remove the whiskers.

The weather-resistant coat is another feature essential to a working dog. The coat keeps cold and wetness away from the body, and its medium length prevents mud, snow or ice

Trimming a fluffy coat does not make it any more acceptable. The fluffy pictured here with a littermate has had its ears trimmed. (Photo by Millie Williams)

from clinging and building up. This is one of the reasons a fluffy coat is a very serious fault. A fluffy coat is softer as well as longer, and it is much more apt to collect and hold debris and to mat or tangle.

COLOR The outer coat is to be of self-colors in red, sable, fawn, black, and tan with or without white markings. White is acceptable on legs, chest, neck (either in part or as a collar), muzzle, underparts, and as a narrow blaze on head. Very serious faults: Whitelies—body color white, with red or dark markings.

Bluies: Colored portions of the coat have a distinct bluish or smoky cast. This coloring is associated with extremely light or blue eyes, liver or gray eye rims, and nose and lip pigment. Mismarks: Self colors with any area of white on the back between withers and tail, on side between elbows and back of hindquarters, or on ears. Black with white markings and no tan present.

The red color that is allowed can range from a very pale honey shade to a very deep, rich red. Sable is red hair tipped with black. Tricolors either can be black with tan over the eyes, on the muzzle and at the tops of the legs, with or without white markings; or can be what is called a "red-headed" tri, having markings more like a Beagle—red and white with a black saddle. Individuals may have their preferences, but no color is officially favored over any other.

This Llanelly tricolor has a minimal amount of white. All black-and-tan dogs are allowed, but black and white as a combination is not. Tan must be present over the eyes and on the cheeks. (Photo by Lucy E. Jones, DVM)

The red color that is allowed by the standard can range from a very pale honey shade to a very deep, rich red. (Photo by Gail Painter)

MOVEMENT IN THE SHOW RING

GAIT Free and smooth. Forelegs should reach well forward without too much lift, in unison with the driving action of the hind legs. The correct shoulder assembly and well-fitted elbows allow a long, free stride in front. Viewed from the front, legs do not move in exact parallel planes, but incline slightly inward to compensate for shortness of leg and width of chest. Hind legs should drive well under the body and move on a line with the forelegs, with hocks turning neither in nor out. Feet must travel parallel to the line of motion with no tendency to swing out, cross over, or interfere with each other. Short, choppy movement, rolling or high-stepping gait, close or overly wide coming or going all are incorrect. This is a herding dog, which must have the agility, freedom of movement and endurance to do the work for which he was developed.

Once again, the emphasis is on correct movement. Reread the last sentence in the preceding paragraph—it says it all.

TEMPERAMENT

TEMPERAMENT Outlook bold, but kindly. Never shy or vicious. The judge shall dismiss from the ring any Pembroke Welsh Corgi that is excessively shy.

Corgis are by nature outgoing, friendly, curious and sometimes courageous to the point of courting danger. A Corgi may be a bit aloof with strangers but should not be shy. No dog should be vicious, and certainly not a Corgi. The well-bred Corgi sees the world as a pleasant, interesting place and is eager to explore strange situations and to meet new people.

No Corgi is perfect, and the conscientious breeder breeds to correct any faults and to strengthen and continue areas that are correct. While a breeder may favor some superficial areas, such as a darker red coat or black-headed tris, all good breeders use the standard as a blueprint for breeding. They are continually striving for correct body proportions, good movement and stable temperament. A Corgi built to the standard will be a healthy, cheerful and willing companion whether it is in the breed ring, competing in a performance event, working as a therapy or service dog, or just being someone's best friend.

A happy, fluffy puppy cuddles with an equally fluffy toy. (Photo by Irma Hilts)

Sunrunners A Kodak Moment. (Photo by Martha Ihrman)

CHAPTER 4

Finding the Right Pembroke Welsh Corgi

I f you've done your homework and determined that a Pembroke Welsh Corgi is the right breed for you, then the next logical step is to get a puppy or an adult dog. This is where you should take a deep breath and slow down.

First, a word about registration papers. People may try to impress you by assuring you that the dog is "AKC registered" or "has papers." All this means is that both of the dog's parents were the same breed. It is not a guarantee of quality. It just guarantees that you have a purebred. Good or bad depends on other factors, not on papers.

A puppy purchased in a pet shop, for example, will have "papers." Its parents will both be Pembroke Welsh Corgis. But that is as much of a guarantee as you will get. You will not get a copy of the pedigree. The parents may or may not meet the standard. Because you can't see them, you will never know. You will not know if they have been tested for hereditary diseases or how close the relationship between them is. (Mother and son? Brother and sister?) There will be no health record and, more importantly, no breeder to ask questions of and learn from.

All puppies are cute, but you should wait until you find the right puppy for your family. (Photo by Winter/Churchill)

It's all too easy to find a dog in pet shops or from classifieds or from the people down the block. But you owe it to yourself, your family and your future puppy to wait to get a happy, healthy dog that fits your lifestyle. This is where the importance of a dedicated breeder comes in.

A dedicated breeder may have multiple litters in a year or may have only one litter every three years. A dedicated breeder is not measured by how many puppies are bred, but by what quality of pups are produced. A dedicated breeder seeks to breed out faults and breed in strengths, and wants healthy, good-tempered pups that will live long lives and be a delight to their owners. A dedicated breeder will ask as many questions of you as you ask of her, and will have a contract drawn up to spell out responsibilities on each side. This breeder also will know enough about the dogs' line and temperament that, whether the puppies are formally tested for temperament or not, she will be able to help you choose the puppy right for you.

For instance, an energetic, bossy puppy may be just the thing for an experienced show or performance home, but it might drive a first-time Corgi owner crazy. In this case, the breeder might suggest a puppy that is more laid-back—or perhaps that bossy pup will be just the right playmate for the children in the family. Listen to the breeder—an expert wants everyone involved to be happy, including the puppy.

HOW TO FIND A GOOD BREEDER

Where do you find this wonderful breeder? You can contact your local all-breed kennel club and see if anyone owns or breeds Corgis. Sometimes local clubs leave a list of breeders at area veterinarians' offices. You also can write or call the American Kennel Club (900-407-7877) and ask for the name and number of the secretary of the Pembroke Welsh Corgi Club of America. The secretary can send you information on the Corgi, including a list of breeders. Or, try the PWCCA's Web page, at www.pembrokecorgi.org, for the same information.

Another source of names is a dog-show catalog. Attending a show also enables you to see the

Responsible breeders put a lot of time into their litters. (Photo by Susan Ewing)

about the breed, though, and possibly will even invite you to see a few dogs. If you haven't seen too many Corgis, this can be a good education. The breeder also might refer you to someone else who might have puppies. Corgi people know other Corgi people, and they all stay in touch.

Passing Your Test

Responsible breeders put a lot of time into their litters, and they will ask many questions. Don't be put off by the questions. A breeder wants what's best for the puppy she has produced. She may have had a bad experience in the past that makes her demand a fenced yard, in spite of your assurance that the dog will never be off lead and will be walked frequently. Be patient and answer honestly. Questions may include how you intend to exercise the puppy: with daily walks, a fenced yard or a kennel run. They will want to know the ages of your children, if any. They also will want to know who the primary caregiver will be. They probably will have conditions attached to the sale as well, such as returning the dog to them if you are unable to keep it. If the dog is sold as a pet, it likely will involve the condition that you spay or neuter the dog.

dogs from that kennel and possibly talk to the owner or handler about them. Names gotten from any of these sources are not a guarantee, but they do indicate that theses breeders are serious enough about the breed that they have put in years raising and showing Corgis and learning about their chosen breed.

Don't expect that the first person you call will have puppies at that moment. You may be put on a waiting list, or the breeder may not have anything to offer at all. She may be willing to talk to you

Many breeders withhold registration papers until proof of spay or neuter is received, or they may sign a limited registration, which means that any offspring of that dog is ineligible to be registered with the AKC. If the puppy is a show prospect, the owner may sell it with the condition

Hang on—Corgi puppies are champion wigglers. (Photo by Susan Ewing)

Look at the mother as well as the puppies before selecting one. (Photo by Susan Ewing)

that you show the puppy, or the breeder may require a co-ownership, with you and the breeder both owning the dog until it achieves its Championship.

Many types of agreements exist, including those in which the breeder agrees to show the dog. Whatever agreement you have, though, get everything in writing and make sure that both sides are clear about the terms. Be sure to think the contract through as well. If the breeder expects you to show the dog, but you are not comfortable with that idea, select another puppy or another breeder. Talk everything through before the sale:

It's better to know up front than to have questions after the money has changed hands.

Screening the Breeder

The breeder has expectations of you as the purchaser, and you should have expectations of the breeder. The puppies should be living in a clean area and should themselves be clean. They should be lively and healthy looking; their eyes should be clear and bright, and their nails should be clipped. They also should be curious about you and willing to be picked up. (Hang on tight—Corgi puppies are champion wigglers!)

Before selecting a dog, look at the mother as well as the puppies. If the sire is on the premises, ask to see him as well. Are any other relatives of the puppies present? Meeting these adults should give you an idea of what your puppy will look and act like when it grows up.

The breeder should have health records for the puppy, including a record of worming and vaccinations. The breeder also should tell you whether the parents have been tested for the blood disorder von Willebrand's disease and whether they have been tested for eye (CERF) and hip (OFA) anomalies. Sometimes the breeder will guarantee the puppy's health in the contract for a certain period of time, usually long enough for you to take the puppy to your own veterinarian.

In recent years, some legislation has been suggested that would make a breeder guarantee the health of the puppy for a year or longer. Most breeders are against this, however, not because they are selling unhealthy puppies, but because they have no control over the puppy after it is sold. An owner who fails to vaccinate, who feeds poor-quality food, and who either overexercises the dog or offers it no exercise at all can hardly blame the breeder for the dog's poor health.

If the sire is on the premises, ask to see him as well. This is Brookshire Royal Flush, OA, with his daughter, Rojanway Summer Fling. (Photo by Carla DeDominicis)

What to Take with You

Finally, you've found a breeder you like, who also likes you. You've both answered each other's questions satisfactorily, money has changed hands and the contract is signed. You both should have a copy of the contract, and you should have your puppy's pedigree, as well as the registration papers or an understanding of when the papers will be received. The breeder also should give you a list of when and what to feed the puppy and should provide a small supply of the food the puppy is currently eating. You should start the puppy off eating the same food, to prevent digestive upset, and you can gradually add a new dog food if you plan to switch brands.

The breeder also may give you the puppy's favorite toy, or a small collar. The breeder probably will encourage you to use a crate and might even include one in the puppy price. You also should make sure that you get the breeder's phone

Puppies' eyes should be clear and bright. This is Ch. Valley-vixen Sunrunner as a puppy. (Photo by Martha Ihrman)

These dogs obviously have a happy, safe home. Many Corgis are not so lucky, however, and end up in a rescue situation. (Photo by Winter/Churchill)

number to keep in a handy place in case you have questions later.

This last item is one of the enormous benefits of buying from a responsible breeder and not from a pet shop. That breeder will be there for you when you have any questions regarding health, grooming or training. A good breeder maintains an interest in every puppy he produces and wants to help you become a good owner. Maintain a good relationship with your breeder; it is priceless.

AN OLDER DOG OR A RESCUE DOG

Almost everyone enjoys a puppy and the chance to bond with a young dog for its entire life, but sometimes an older dog makes more sense. A person may not have the time—or the energy—that a puppy demands. For example, an older person may find an older dog much easier to live with.

The search for an older dog is similar to that for a puppy. Talk to reputable breeders in your area. They may have a retired Champion they would consider placing in a pet home, or, maybe they kept a puppy as a show prospect and it didn't work out. This is your chance to obtain a socialized, trained dog that will not make the time and energy demands that a puppy does. Of course, you should approach your search for a breeder in the same manner as you would when seeking a puppy, and you still should be given a contract and health records.

Another source of an older dog is through a rescue organization. Almost all national purebred clubs have a rescue organization, and the Pembroke Welsh Corgi Club of America is no exception. Check with the AKC for the name of its rescue coordinator, who will refer you to someone in your area who can help you. If you're in an area that has a regional Corgi Club, you will be referred there.

A rescued Corgi is one that, for one reason or another, has lost its original home. It may be that divorce or death has left the dog homeless, or the dog may have been found running loose or has been turned in to an animal shelter. In such a case, someone who is familiar with Corgis and who can determine what kind of family the dog needs provides a foster home for the dog and evaluates it for adoption. Is the dog good with other animals and with children? Have any injuries or illnesses affected the dog? Is it terrified of vacuum cleaners?

Before a rescue dog is placed, it is examined by a veterinarian, spayed or neutered and brought up to date on shots, a big plus for the new owner. Also on the plus side when adopting a rescued Corgi is that the dog might already be trained (and housetrained) to some extent. *Older* may mean *calmer* as well.

On the negative side, a rescued dog's history is unknown most of the time. You won't always know what to expect in any given situation, although the rescue committee will have evaluated the dog's personality as well as possible while it was in foster care. Still, knowing that you're giving a home to a dog that really needs one may outweigh any negatives.

Don't be surprised, though, if the rescue coordinator asks as many (or more) questions as a breeder placing a puppy. This dog has already lost one home, and the rescue worker wants to make sure that this time, it's for keeps. Also, don't expect a rescued dog to be free. A lot of time and expense goes into the rescue dog, from a spay or neuter to vaccinations, to transportation, to housing and food.

Your support makes it possible for the rescue committee to meet expenses and to continue its efforts to find and place homeless Corgis.

Wherever you get your Corgi, and however old it is, remember that it is a commitment for the life of the dog. Your Corgi will give you unconditional love; it deserves the best you can give in return.

SAMPLE CONTRACTS

Contracts can be as simple or as complex as either party considers necessary. More detail is probably better, but here are four samples.

Received from _____
the amount of $ _____
for one Pembroke Welsh Corgi puppy,
out of _____ by _____.

Above male puppy is fully guaranteed for a period of 30 days from date of sale, provided good physical care is given in the interim.

Breeder reserves the right to use said dog at stud with breeder's own bitches, provided he grows to be a desirable animal for such a purpose. AKC papers will be provided when available.

Sample 1.

Special Notations

Definitions

Pet: A companion animal purebred and AKC-registerable that is sold as a pet with no warranty that the dog will be show-quality or breeding stock.

Showable: A puppy or adult that goes beyond and above the definition of a pet dog. This animal must be free of all disqualifying faults. This dog is in no way guaranteed to win in the show ring unless this is agreed to in writing in this contract at the time of execution. It is understood that, with proper care on the part of the Buyer, in due time the dog should be of acceptable temperament and structure, and should embody the basic standard of the breed.

Show: An animal that has all the qualifications of showable, plus being one that, with proper handling, can and should win in the conformation ring. If there are any further guarantees, they must be in writing.

Agreement of Sale

Date _____

Name of Purchaser_____

Address _____

Telephone_____

Name of Seller_____

Address _____

Telephone_____

The following dog _____of Pembroke Welsh Corgi breed, on this _____ day of_____in the year_____has been sold to the person or persons listed above as purchaser and is free of any liens or encumbrances as a result of stud fee, veterinary fees, etc.

Description of Dog:

Sex_____ Age_____

Colors_____Litter registration no. _____

•If within forty-eight hours of the date of sale you believe the dog to be sick, you agree to return it to us and we will refund the purchase price or return the dog to you well, if you so desire. If, however, you take the dog to the veterinarian during this period, or incur any expense, the seller shall not be responsible.

•This agreement is made for our mutual benefit—to protect you as well as ourselves—and we wish it understood that, under no circumstances will we stand responsible after forty-eight hours, or if any expense is incurred in connection with the care of this dog through veterinary bills during this forty-eight hour period. Exceptions will be made for recognized holidays.

•Any deletions to this contract shall be struck out and initialed by both parties, and additional amendments will be noted on the back of this agreement, followed by the signature of both parties.

Sample 2.

CONTRACT OF SALE

(Kennel name)
(Address)
(Phone number)

Purchaser_____

Address_____

Phone_____

The sale of a Pembroke Welsh Corgi (color and sex) Whelped _____ AKC litter no. _____ Name _____ is made upon the following terms and conditions.

1) Full purchase price of $_____ to be paid upon receipt of above described Corgi.

2) Breeder/seller has provided purchaser with AKC papers when paid by cash or certified check. If paid by check, papers to follow when check clears.

3) This Corgi puppy is sold as a show potential puppy, which means that her type and conformation and temperament follow the standard of this breed, and that she has no disqualifying faults at this time.

   If this puppy does not live up to her show potential in the opinion of seller, purchaser and one additional Corgi breeder, purchaser may have her spayed and keep her, or have her spayed and sell her to a home agreed to by breeder/seller.

4) This puppy is being sold for seller's pet price. If purchaser wishes to breed her to a dog of seller's choice, seller will be given one puppy of seller's choice from resulting litter. Puppy to be selected by seller at 10 to 12 weeks of age.

5) If at any time in the future, purchaser is unable to keep this dog, purchaser agrees to return her to seller with AKC papers signed back to seller with no monies exchanged, or place or sell her to a suitable home agreed to by seller. She must first be spayed at purchaser's expense.

Purchaser agrees never to give this puppy to a shelter or relinquish her to a puppy mill, pet shop or sell her out of this country.

I hereby accept the terms and conditions of this sale.

Purchaser_____

Seller_____

Date _____

Sample 3.

SALES CONTRACT

(Kennel Name)

Whereas _____ hereinafter called "Seller" is the owner of a (show/showable/pet) Pembroke Welsh Corgi (dog/bitch) further described as:

Registered Name of Dog _____

Litter Registration No. _____

Name and Registration No. of Sire _____

Name and Registration No. of Dam _____

and whereas _____ hereinafter called "Buyer" is desirous of purchasing the animal described above.

Now, therefore, in consideration of the sum of $ _____ dollars, the Seller hereby conveys one (show/showable/pet) Pembroke Welsh Corgi (dog/bitch) under the following warranties and conditions and no other warranties or conditions either expressed or implied.

1. That the above described animal is a purebred dog, registerable with the AKC and that a registration application or individual registration, has been given to Buyer as of the date of purchase, EXCEPT AS FOLLOWS:
   A. Pet quality animal, or limited registrations.
   B. Buyer of Pet animal agrees to neuter such animal. _____ (Buyer)

2. That the above described animal may for any reason be returned prepaid to Seller within seven (7) days or as otherwise agreed in writing at the time of receipt. Buyer shall assume full responsibility for the health, anatomical make-up, appearance and temperament of the above-described animal during said 7 days. If the condition of the animal has changed in any of the categories mentioned in the previous sentence, the Seller is relieved of obligation to return the full amount of the purchase price, otherwise the full purchase price will be refunded.

3. Seller reserves a LIFETIME RIGHT OF FIRST REFUSAL if Buyer can no longer keep above described animal. _____ Buyer)

WHEREFORE, the above named Seller and Buyer have executed the foregoing contract of sale at _____(a.m./p.m.) on this day of _____ 19____ at _____ .

State of _____

_____(Buyer, address and phone no.)

_____(Seller, address and phone no.)

Sample 4.

(Photo by Lucy E. Jones, DVM)

CHAPTER 5

Living with Your Pembroke Welsh Corgi

The best time to bring home a new puppy is on a weekend or during a vacation so that it will have lots of time to get used to its new home before the routines of work and school interfere. The *worst* time to bring home a new puppy is Christmas.

Of course, the idea of a Christmas puppy is hard to resist, especially when so many Christmas cards show puppies under a tree. In reality, even though someone may be home over the holidays, the excitement and activity can negate that benefit. There may be so many activities that the puppy is neglected—or else never left alone to rest. During the holidays, there also are more chances for the puppy to eat things it shouldn't: electrical cords, decorative tinsel and chocolate, to name a few. What's more, people get stressed at the holidays—imagine how an 8-week-old puppy will feel!

In fact, most breeders refuse to sell a puppy just before the holidays. If you still want the puppy to be a holiday gift, give a certificate stating that the puppy may be picked up after the first of the year. Put a lead, collar and training books under the tree, and wait for a calmer time to bring home the puppy.

Puppies are adorable on Christmas cards . . .

. . . if you can get them to hold still! (Photos by Carla DeDominicis)

THE MANY USES OF A CRATE

When you've brought your wonderful Corgi puppy home, it's time for you to learn to live with each other. Hopefully you thought ahead and got the puppy his own bowls, the right food, a light collar and lead and, of course, a crate.

Add some towels to the crate so your puppy has a soft place to rest, give him some toys to play with, attach a water bowl to the crate door or side, and your puppy—and later your adult dog—has a safe, enjoyable place to stay when you can't supervise his activities. I recommend attaching the water bowl to a door or wall of the crate because

otherwise the odds are good that the puppy will tip over any regular bowl. You may also want to feed your puppy in the crate, so that he associates something positive with being separated from the family.

New owners frequently look upon a crate as a small jail or a prison. Instead, it should be looked at as the dog sees it: as a den, a safe haven from the sometimes-confusing human world. A crate also is a wonderful way to keep a curious puppy safe when you are not there to supervise him. With your new puppy safe in his crate, you can go out for a few hours without worrying about your Persian rug or whether your puppy is teething on an electrical cord. Using a crate also means that if the puppy relieves himself in the crate, the mess is in a small, easy-to-clean space, not in the middle of the new beige carpet.

When the dog gets older, the crate will still be his den, his safe place. If you have company or a party, crating your dog keeps him safe and your guests happy. You don't have to worry that your dog will dart out the door as people arrive or leave. The dog won't ruin the lovely tray of hors d'oeuvres left temptingly on the coffee table or be fed too many treats by well-meaning visitors. Also, people who are not dog lovers, or who may be allergic, will not have to spend their time avoiding your pet, brushing dog hair from their pants or worrying about runs in their stockings from an enthusiastic greeting from the dog. If small children visit and you can't supervise dog and child interaction, a crate keeps everyone happy and safe.

As an added bonus, a crate protects your dog in the car and keeps him in one place, not bouncing around in the vehicle. A crate is a real bonus while traveling as well; relatives may be more receptive to your furry pal if he's crated, and most motels definitely are. Besides assuring that your dog will not destroy room furnishings if left alone, there's no chance that a crated dog will escape when the housekeeper arrives to clean the room.

Crates of Many Shapes and Sizes

Crates come in all varieties, which offer their own advantages. Some are folding wire crates that are compact and easy to carry; others are sturdy plastic

The idea is to sleep inside the crate, not on top of it. (Photo by Lucy E. Jones, DVM)

"airline" models. Wire crates should have a cover to create the den effect, but the advantage of a wire crate is that the sides of the cover can be flipped up to allow for more air circulation in hot weather.

When you're shopping for a crate, remember that it needs to be large enough for your dog to stretch out lying down and should be roomy enough for the dog to also be able to turn around easily. Too big, and it defeats the purpose of a den

Sometimes even a crate won't keep away the outside world. (Photo by Lucy E. Jones, DVM)

A breeder will often begin crate-training puppies before they leave for their new homes. (Photo by Irma Hilts)

(cozy and protecting). During housetraining, a too-large crate also makes it possible for the puppy to use one end as a bed and the other end as a bathroom, which defeats the crate's usefulness as a housetraining tool. Because Corgis are short, you will end up with a crate that gives you more head room than you need in order to accommodate the Corgi's length lying down. You might want to consider a smaller crate for housetraining, or block off part of a larger, adult-size crate to make training easier.

The initial expense may seem high ($50 to $80), but a crate will last for more than a lifetime, and the benefits definitely make it worth the cost.

So, invest in a crate. Not only is it invaluable as a housetraining tool (more on this later), but it also keeps your dog safe, is a refuge for the dog and serves as the dog's den.

Rules for Crate-Training

Having said that, the crate, like any tool, can also be abused. A crate definitely is not to be used for 24-hour-a-day confinement. Your dog—especially a puppy—needs time to play, time to explore and time to interact with the family. Set a schedule for housetraining, with regular visits to the backyard, but also make sure that the puppy has time to become a part of the family.

Your puppy will adjust more easily if he can sleep in your room at night. For one thing, he won't feel so lonely, and for eight hours or more, he will be with you, with no effort on your part. Also, you'll hear him if he whines and needs to go outside in the middle of the night. For this reason, you may want to get two crates—one for the bedroom, and one for the kitchen, the family room or wherever your puppy can be part of the family activity, yet out of the way when no one can watch him.

HOUSETRAINING YOUR CORGI

As mentioned earlier, crate training is the easiest and most direct way to housetrain a puppy, for two main reasons. One reason is that dogs don't like to soil their beds. Given a chance, they will go somewhere else. Puppies learn quickly that if they wait, they will be taken somewhere else. Another advantage of using a crate is that it prevents accidents. Dogs have a very good sense of smell, and that sense of smell guides them back to areas where they've "gone" and they are likely to "go" again. It's very hard to eliminate all odor from a carpet, which means the puppy will find that same spot again and again. Using a crate means that you take the puppy out to the correct spot in the yard, instead of the puppy's choosing a spot indoors. Take the puppy out right after naps, shortly after meals and after play periods. Each time, take the puppy to the same spot in the yard, and praise him

Puppies are fast—and small enough to scoot almost anywhere. (Photo by Carla DeDominicis)

when he eliminates. Have a schedule, and stick to it—the puppy will soon get used to the schedule. If everyone is away during the day, try to make arrangements to come home at noon at least for the first few weeks. If that's not possible, check with a neighbor or their child to set up some sort of arrangement to let the dog out.

Most Corgi puppies will sleep through the night if taken out between 10 P.M. and 11 P.M., and then in the morning between 6 A.M. and 7 A.M. If the bedroom is cool and the puppy seems to be waking you in the middle of the night, try adding more bedding to keep him warmer. Like people, when a puppy gets cold, he wakes up and has to go out.

While crate-training is the easiest, quickest method of housetraining, in some situations this might not be possible. If your schedule doesn't permit, or if you live in an apartment in which quick trips out are not possible, paper training will work. Paper training follows the same principle as taking your puppy to the same spot outside each time. Use a very heavy layer of paper; when you notice your puppy circling and sniffing, rush him to the paper. Praise the puppy when he goes. Then remove the top layers of paper, and replace them with fresh paper. Make sure that enough scent of urine remains, however, to guide the puppy the next time. Gradually reduce the size of the area that the paper covers.

If you will not be present to supervise, use a small area that can be enclosed, such as a bathroom or a corner of a kitchen barricaded with an excerise pen (ex-pen). Place the puppy's crate in this area, too. Cover the area with papers, and gradually reduce the area as suggested previously.

If you are an apartment dweller and want to continue to have an indoor bathroom for your dog, consider some kind of a litter-box arrangement. A Corgi is a bit large for a cat box, but something of that kind would work.

In spite of all your precautions, of course, your Corgi probably will have an accident or two on the carpet. White vinegar, club soda and lots of paper towels will take care of the problem: Club soda prevents staining, and white vinegar neutralizes the smell of urine so that the puppy is not encouraged to return to that spot. Never use ammonia-based cleaner, however, because there is ammonia in urine—that smell just reinforces the area as a good place for the puppy to go. Pour on

the white vinegar, and then make a pad of paper towels—use six or seven, and fold them as small as you can and still cover the spot. Place the towels over the spot, and stand on it—press hard. Repeat with fresh paper towels until the towels are no longer absorbing anything. (Owning stock in a paper-towel company while you're housetraining your puppy will make the number of towels you use less painful.)

Another handy cleaning tool is a regular paper plate. A healthy dog's stool is usually firm enough to pick up easily with a baggie, just as you would do on a walk. If, however, the dog has a touch of diarrhea, or vomits, a paper plate makes a great "scoop." Just fold the plate in half, firmly crease along the fold and use the straight edge to push under the mess.

REQUIRED EQUIPMENT

Through all this, unless you have a fenced yard, always take your puppy out on a lead. Even with a fenced yard, a lead is a good idea. Puppies are faster than you might think, and their size makes it possible for them to scoot under bushes and shrubs easily. You can probably still catch your puppy at this age, but if you're dressed for work and the puppy is enjoying the mud under the lilac bush, you'll wish you'd kept him controlled on a lead walking on the clean grass. The puppy should be wearing a light buckle collar, and even a show lead will keep everyone happy and not be too heavy for a young dog. As the puppy matures, you can think about training collars and different leads, but for now, something light will make going out a less-stressful event.

For your dog's indoor comfort, you'll find all kinds of dog dishes on the market, some with their own cute mats. Stainless steel is always a good material, as is hard-molded plastic or ceramic (but be sure that the glaze is not lead-based). Plastic and stainless steel probably rank as the better choices, though, because you don't have to worry about breakage. Whatever kind you use, take up the bowl and wash it after each meal. I have never understood how anyone could leave a dog dish down meal after meal, sometimes with leftover food encrusted. (Although, I admit, with a Corgi, leftover food is not likely.) The same goes for the water bowl. Fresh, clean water in a clean bowl should always be available. Your dog is never going to ask for a pair of expensive sneakers or money for the prom, so give him the proper basics.

On the subject of water bowls, I'm not sure what happens when a Corgi has only a small bowl because the dogs at our house drink from a large communal bowl, a legacy from our first dog, who weighed in at 110 pounds. This large bowl has always been an invitation to stick front feet in and paddle. At least three of our Corgis have done this, although one outgrew it when he became an adult. Currently, our 6-year-old male considers it the fastest way to cool off. After a fast game of tag with the youngest, he will splash vigorously with his front feet, wetting his underside and swamping the kitchen floor. If I can catch him before he starts, we go outside—I fill a large, shallow, plastic litter box with water and he jumps in and out of

Your dog will appreciate a clean bowl for his meals. (Photo by Winter/Churchill)

that. If I don't catch him—well, it's amazing how much water one bath towel can soak up.

While your dog is a puppy, you probably will be using towels or paper as bedding—something cheap, easily replaceable or easily washable in the case of towels. As the puppy matures, the siren call of designer beds will be heard. My advice is to resist this call. Wicker baskets, while charming, seem to invite total destruction by chewing. "Beanbag" beds filled with tiny white beans of

This furry companion is ready for any adventure. (Photo by Lucy E. Jones, DVM)

polystyrene are fine until a seam splits. We had an old beanbag chair that the Corgis all loved, but the seams started to split—and, for some reason, the Corgis (especially my youngest) liked eating the beans. They were apparently harmless, but it's a little disconcerting to go into the yard to poop-scoop and find piles of white beans!

Other dog beds may have removable covers over a foam rubber or polyfill core. These are very appealing, and the covers are indeed easy to wash, but no matter what the core is made of, it takes forever to dry when it gets washed. The one bed I own that has a "holofil" inner mattress has a tag that says, "Do not wash, do not dry clean. Spot clean only." Right—a dog bed you can't wash. I do wash it, but, as mentioned, it takes forever to dry. Remember also that if you have a dog that settles down for a good chew and ignores all the wonderful toys for a corner of the bed, it can get expensive to replace.

Some of the newer dog beds on the market do have machine-washable cushions, many with baffles or quilting so that the stuffing doesn't bunch or shift. Check the labels. If you have only one dog, you might want a fancier bed in the living room or family room.

Our one large dog bed with the washable cover and the "holofil" core is in the living room for whatever dog gets to it first. In all the crates, I have beds made of various layers of old flannel sheets, thick towels and fluffy pieces of synthetic fleece. These make warm, soft beds that the dogs can nest in if they want to, and all the parts are easily washable and dryable. It's easy to add more material in the winter and remove some in the summer.

So far, this chapter has covered the basics needed to introduce your Corgi to your household safely and easily. It has suggested possibilities for beds, food, crates, water, leads, collars and vaccinations. What it can't cover completely is all the funny, irritating, wonderful things Corgis do every day that make it almost impossible for a Corgi person to think of owning any other breed.

Because the Pembroke Welsh Corgi is a purebred, there are certain traits that each Corgi will share with every other. But, Corgis are also individuals. Each dog's personality will come through and will be different from every other.

Brecon, our first male, was very independent. He felt he knew best in every situation. While we did attend obedience classes, and he would heel, do sit and down stays and do a recall, he would not do an automatic sit. When heeling with a dog, the dog is supposed to automatically sit at your side when you stop moving. Brecon would not. He would stop, but he would always remain standing. I think he wanted to be alert and ready for whatever was next. I never trusted Brecon off-lead. He was too willing to go his own way. As a watch dog, he was a moderate barker. He definitely barked when people came to the door, but not much more than that.

Many dogs have a sense of time and will know exactly when dinner is, or when someone should be coming home. Brecon knew that 10 P.M. was

Some dogs (and their owners) prefer recliners to commercial dog beds. (Photo by Susan Ewing)

bedtime, but instead of just going upstairs by himself, if we had company, he would sit in front of them and stare, trying to make them go home.

Our current male, Griffin, also has a keen sense of time, but he is more vocal about it. When my mother's husband died, she frequently came to our house for dinner, leaving each evening at about 7:20. Griffin soon learned the pattern, and now, if my mother is visiting, he starts to bark at her at 7:20. The only remedy is putting him in his crate until after she leaves.

He barks frequently. He barks whenever he hears a noise outside that is strange. He barks when people come to the door. He barks, I believe, when a leaf falls to the ground.

He also has had his share of obedience lessons, but again, I would never trust him off-lead outdoors.

Megan, on the other hand, never had a single obedience lesson, yet I could trust her off lead. If we were in the park and she ran after a flock of birds, she would immediately return when I called her. She was also the only dog I've ever had that did not like her crate. She would sometimes go into a crate on her own, but if she were shut in, she would start to pant and get very stressed. She was a beautiful Corgi and did win show points in both the United States and Canada, but she hated to show, so we never finished her.

Megan barked for no reason at all. Sometimes she would just lay in the middle of the living room and bark. I never heard her howl, but my parents said that when we left her with them and went out, she would howl until we came home.

Hayley was more mature at 6 months than Griffin was at 5 years. She is a gentle, soft dog who rarely needs a correction, and when she does, a little quiet direction does the trick. She loves laps and cuddling. She only barks when she wants Griffin to play, although she will occasionally howl. She will retrieve, but not for long; she'd rather play with the ball by herself, nudging it away, and then pouncing on it.

All Corgis, and all with similarities and differences. Almost all tried to "herd" me when they were puppies, by biting at my ankles. All have enjoyed sleeping on their backs, with their feet in the air. The thick, double coat has meant tufts of hair from them all. They have all been chow hounds. Beyond that, they have all had individual personalities and I have loved them all for their differences. Did I ever have a favorite? They were, and are, all my favorites, for different reasons. You can't replace a Corgi who has died, but you can enjoy a new one for itself.

MULTIPLE CORGIS

It frequently happens that one Corgi, like one potato chip, is not enough. Corgis seem to manage quite well as a pack, but caution is advised. Not all the dogs will like all the other dogs all the time. My first male was fairly laid-back when it came to other males. Griffin and his brother Balin always got along fine, but they were always on neutral ground when his owner and I shared a motel room at a dog show. What would have happened had Balin entered Griffin's home, or vice versa, I don't know. I do know that Griffin barely tolerated the introduction of Merlin into the house, and

Merlin was a 10-year-old neutered male. As Griffin matured, the rivalry grew worse until, finally, they could no longer be loose together.

Megan and Heather were fine loose, but if they were crated for feeding, or in the car while riding, the uncrating had to be done carefully, or they would fight. Usually, Heather was let out first and taken some distance away, and then Megan was released. If Megan was released first, she would charge Heather's crate, growling and snarling.

With multiple dogs in the family, it is a good idea to make sure each dog has its own crate. Putting two dogs in one crate may work for awhile, but sooner or later, one dog will push the other too far, and in a closed crate, there is no room for either dog to escape.

Many people live with multiple Corgis, so it is not impossible, but it does require caution, commonsense and a knowledge of each dog's personality and temperament.

By this time, you've supplied the essentials: food, water, safety, a bed, play time, nap time, patience and love. In return, you've got a furry companion who will always be ready for whatever adventure you offer. Just don't forget to sign up for some obedience lessons!

Am./Can. Ch. Valleyvixen Don Juan.
(Photo courtesy of Martha and Don Ihrman)

CHAPTER 6

Keeping Your Pembroke Welsh Corgi Happy and Healthy

The first and best thing you can do for your Corgi's health is to find and use a veterinarian that you trust. As with human doctors, all veterinarians are not alike. No matter how qualified the professional is, if you don't like his manner or his staff's manner, you will not feel comfortable taking your dog to that clinic.

Talk to other dog owners to see what veterinarians they like and why. Have they had problems with anyone? If they have a complaint, is it legitimate? Sometimes, of course, you won't like a particular veterinarian, even though he or she comes highly recommended. If that is the case, find another doctor. You need to feel confident and happy with your choice.

Think about the services that you want from a veterinarian. Maybe proximity is important in your choice, or maybe you feel more comfortable in a practice with multiple doctors. Think carefully; this is not a decision to be made lightly.

The first and best thing you can do for your Corgi's health is to find a veterinarian whom you trust. (Photo by Winter/Churchill)

Also look for a veterinarian who has emergency access, who will talk to you about a problem if you call and who has a staff that will not brush you off if you say that you have an emergency. Look for a veterinarian who understands that he or she is treating you as the owner, as well as treating your dog. The first veterinarian I had in Vermont years ago understood that. In one instance, I had called after office hours about something, and after the veterinarian listened to me, he said, "The dog can wait until morning, but can you?" He met me at his office in 20 minutes.

Today, I probably would have waited, but I still appreciate a veterinarian who responds to my concerns.

SPAYING AND NEUTERING

The most important words on spaying or neutering are these: *Do it.*

Neither of these operations is difficult or particularly hard on a healthy, young dog. Neutering is the easier of the two because the testicles are external. After the veterinarian anesthetizes the animal, an incision is made at the base of the scrotum, the testicles are removed and the incision is stitched up. Most veterinarians will keep your dog overnight to make sure that he completely recovers from the anesthetic, and that's it. If an owner worries about appearance, the veterinarian will do a vasectomy.

Spaying takes a little longer because it requires abdominal surgery. The dog is anesthetized, and a short incision is made in the abdomen and in the wall of muscle. The doctor draws out the ovaries and the uterus, ties off blood vessels, cuts the uterus and ovaries free, pushes the remaining tissue and fat back into the abdomen and stitches up the incision. Again, the dog will be held overnight for observation. You will need to return in about 10 days to have the stitches removed. During that time, it is a good idea to keep an eye on the incision just in case—redness or puffiness could indicate infection.

Both spaying and neutering offer additional benefits to the animal beyond avoiding unwanted

Your veterinarian can help you decide at what age you should spay or neuter your pet. (Photo by Susan Ewing)

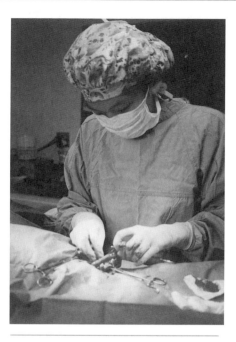

Dr. Sandra Wu performs a spay. (Photo by Susan Ewing)

litters. Spaying a female before her third heat lowers her chance of developing mammary tumors. After the third heat, there is not much difference in the incidence of these tumors, but spaying does end the chance of pyometra, an infection and inflammation of the uterus, usually in older bitches, and hormonally influenced. Pyometra usually leads to infertility, and in severe cases the uterus must be removed. Spaying also eliminates the twice yearly "season."

For intact males, neutering makes them less susceptible to prostatic hypertrophy, which is a benign enlargement of the prostate. Neutering also

prevents general prostate problems and may help in temperament problems, such as aggression and territorial marking inside the house.

As an example of this last point, my male Corgi, Griffin, persisted in lifting his leg against any and all furniture. I showed him until he was about 4, and then I considered having him neutered. I was told that at his age, his behavior patterns were set, and neutering probably would not change his habit of marking. So I left him alone and continued to go through rolls of paper towels and bottles of white vinegar. Then I decided to purchase a puppy bitch to show. I didn't want any accidental litters and also didn't want the hassle of keeping the dogs separated or boarding one when the bitch came in season. So, Griffin was neutered—and he hasn't marked since.

Griffin is still a tornado. He still barks at just about everything, still plays fetch with his tennis ball forever and still defends his bone against the other dogs. He just doesn't mark anymore. Granted, each dog is different, and what is true for my dog may not be for yours. Still, I wish I'd had him neutered sooner. I could have saved a fortune in cleaning supplies.

With both males and females, you may have to watch their weight after spaying and neutering. Metabolism does seem to slow, so even if the dog's activity level remains the same, your Corgi could gain weight. Lucy Jones, a veterinarian and also a Corgi breeder, says that she was told in school that weight gain was a myth, but her own observation with her dogs indicates otherwise.

Most dogs are spayed or neutered when they are at least 6 months old, although many shelters now are practicing early spay and neuters at 8 weeks of age. William Seleen, Jr., DVM, understands why shelters take this approach because it is the best way to decrease surplus population—still, he wonders whether it is in the best interest of the puppy. Will these puppies be smaller than normal? Growth plates close at the onset of hormone production; if no hormones are produced, will growth continue? Is there an increase in Cushing's disease? This has been found to be true in ferrets and mice that have been spayed and neutered at an early age, but not enough research has yet been done with dogs.

Of course, you shouldn't spay or neuter your Corgi if you plan to show the dog. Your dog or bitch must be intact for conformation showing, although they may be neutered and still compete in any of the performance events. If your dog is a pet and you plan a life for it as a full-time companion, however, do everyone a favor— including the dog—and schedule a spay or neuter.

VACCINATIONS

My current veterinarian recommends shots at 12 and 16 weeks of age for puppies, and then annually thereafter. Twelve weeks is the earliest age at which most veterinarians will give the rabies vaccine; the dog should have another at 1 year of age, and then according to your state's law after that. (Rabies vaccinations are required in every state, although each state differs with schedule requirements. Some require an annual rabies vaccination, while others require one only every three years. Your veterinarian will know what your state requires.) Veterinarians typically don't start vaccinations on puppies any younger than 12 weeks because the antibodies they get from their mother negate the vaccines.

Other shots your dog is likely to receive include those to prevent distemper and hepatitis. Your veterinarian may also recommend, or automatically give, a shot for parainfluenza, or "kennel cough." In some regions, protection may also be

Rawhide bones help keep teeth clean. (Photo by Susan Ewing)

suggested against Lyme disease. Consult your veterinarian for the vaccines your dog should have.

Although many veterinarians give the leptospirosis vaccine, mine does not, for two reasons. One is that most shots are given yearly, but the lepto vaccine is effective only for six months. The other is that he has seen adverse reactions to that vaccine. He does give the Corona vaccine, but he leaves it out of a regular vaccination program if it reacts with a particular dog.

TEETH

Dental care is very important because tartar buildup can lead to abscesses, and bacteria can cause pneumonia or heart problems. Take action before a serious problem develops. For starters, choose a good dry food. Although most dogs seem to swallow food without much chewing, dry foods may help remove some plaque from the teeth and are less likely than either canned or semi-moist foods to get packed within gum crevices.

Give your dog chewing material as well to help clean his teeth. Hard dog biscuits do help remove tartar, but studies have shown that rawhide does the job better. Three strips of rawhide daily is "significantly more effective at removing supragingival calculus [plaque] above the gum-line than dry food or biscuits" (*Veterinary Product News*, February 1992). Also effective are synthetic bones made of nylon. These "bones" provide a hard surface for chewing but don't splinter as a real bone might. Instead, as the dog chews, the nylon surface gets rough and almost "bristly," acting like a

toothbrush. The small pieces of nylon that the dog ingests pass harmlessly through the digestive tract. Avoid real bones, however—they can cause damage to teeth or can splinter when chewed, which can cause internal problems if the splinters are swallowed. Dogs sometimes also become ill after eating a lot of bone.

Dr. Edward Eisner, writing in the dental newsletter *The Enamel Pearl*, advises daily tooth brushing to keep food from being trapped in the gums, where it will decay. He also recommends professional cleaning at least once a year.

Talk to your veterinarian about ways to keep your dog's teeth free of tartar and plaque. There are all kinds of brushes, toothpastes and mouthwashes for dogs. Just make sure that what you use is indeed for dogs—human toothpastes and mouthwashes are a no-no because fluoride can build up and poison a dog.

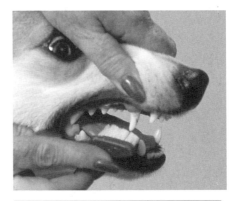

Teach your dog to allow you to check its teeth regularly. (Photo by Winter/Churchill)

PARASITES

A regular fecal check is an easy way to identify internal parasites in your dog before they cause serious harm. Whipworms, roundworms and hookworms can all be discovered in this way. To detect heartworms, your dog must undergo a blood test for detection. Tapeworm segments usually can be seen in the feces directly.

Hookworm eggs are passed in the feces. Contaminated soil is one of the causes of infection; the other is by transmission from the brood bitch to the puppies. Instead of maturing, larvae may remain in the tissues of the bitch and then pass to the mammary glands and infect the pups. Hookworms feed on the blood of their host and can cause fatal anemia in a puppy. Some monthly heartworm prevention, also prevent hookworm.

As with hookworms, roundworms contaminate the soil—the eggs are very resistant to adverse conditions and may remain in the soil for years. Most puppies are born with these worms because the larvae may live in an intermediate host but not infect it. In this case, the larvae leak from the pregnant bitch to the pups and infect them. This is why puppies are de-wormed at an early age.

Whipworms can cause deep inflammation of the wall of the colon, and periodic bouts of diarrhea with mucus and blood can be observed if the infection is heavy. Again, contaminated soil is to blame. Once whipworms are in your soil, paving the entire area is about the only way to totally solve the problem. In treating for whipworms, your veterinarian will prescribe the proper drugs to kill the worms.

Technician and doctor prepare to draw blood for a heartworm test. (Photo by Susan Ewing)

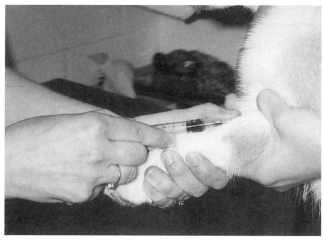

Sometimes finding a vein in short-legged dogs is the hardest part. (Photo by Susan Ewing)

Ch. Elfwish Lyleth. (Photo by Ashbey Photography)

Tapeworms are the most common and the least harmful of the worms dogs may get. Dogs may become infected from eating uncooked meat or from swallowing fleas. If your dog does have tapeworms, your veterinarian will prescribe a medicine to kill them. Controlling the local flea population is one of the best ways to prevent your dog from getting tapeworms.

Heartworm is a deadly parasite that kills or incapacitates dogs it infects. Heartworm larvae develop in mosquitoes and invade the dog when the mosquito bites it. These larvae finally take up residence in the chambers of the right side of the dog's heart. There the worms mature and produce microfilariae, which circulate in the blood until another mosquito ingests them after feeding on the dog. Adult heartworms can completely fill the heart chambers. An infected dog may tire easily and develop a cough. A blood test is required to see if microfilariae are present in the bloodstream, which indicates heartworm infestation.

A dog diagnosed with heartworms is first treated to rid it of the adult worms. This treatment involves arsenamide injected intravenously twice a day for two or three days. The worms die slowly and are carried to the lungs, where they gradually disintegrate. This type of "slow poison" is preferred because if the worms were all killed immediately, simultaneous embolism might prove fatal, and even killing them slowly stresses the lungs. Enforced rest for four to six weeks following treatment is usual to help recovery.

FLEAS

The flea generally seen around dogs is a cat flea that actually came from Africa. Because it is so common, it is becoming resistant to many of the flea-control products on the market today. Vacuuming is as effective as any spray, and daily combing with a flea comb is also an effective way to remove fleas from the dog. Wash bedding frequently because that is where most of the flea eggs will be found.

Fleas seem to develop a resistance to chemical products within five years, but several new products available from your veterinarian are making it easier to maintain a flea prevention plan. Monthly ingested Program is not an insecticide, so it may be used with other products. It acts as a birth control pill for fleas by preventing a cocoon from forming so that the larvae of the flea never mature to adults. Frontline, a monthly topical preventative, also is effective against fleas and also against ticks for 17 days. Amitraz is another effective remedy against ticks, but it can react negatively with other drugs. I also have had very good luck with Advantage, also a monthly topical preventative, and the Corgis seem to tolerate it well.

HEALTH PROBLEMS

Responsible Corgi breeders test their stock and are careful not to breed animals with known hereditary health problems. One of the diseases they may test for is von Willebrand's disease, a blood disorder. Von Willebrand's disease is similiar to hemophilia, except the dog doesn't start bleeding right away if injured, but uses up its limited amount of clotting factor. Once this reduced amount of clotting ability is used, the dog will bleed without clotting. If surgery is necessary and it is known ahead of time that a dog has the disease, plasma can be supplied. Researchers at Michigan State University and the University of Michigan have discovered that a gene mutation is responsible for von Willebrand's disease in Pembroke Welsh Corgis, so it is now possible for a DNA test to determine if a Corgi is affected or is a carrier.

Sources vary on whether back problems are hereditary in Corgis: Some sources say that the dogs have a predilection for disc problems, while others notice no more problems in Corgis than in

Corgis are definitely "chow hounds" and should never be free-fed. Measure the amount of food they eat each day. (Photo by Winter/Churchill)

any other breed. Intervertebral discs are soft, pulpy "cushions" with a gristly outer ring, and they are located between each vertebrae. They act as shock absorbers and support for the spinal cord. If a disc ruptures, either partially or completely, there is a compression of the spinal cord, which causes the dog pain and may cause temporary or permanent paralysis. Disc damage may be caused by jumping, slipping or falling. In many cases, natural recovery occurs within two weeks, although recovery could take longer if paralysis is present. Your veterinarian may prescribe steroids to reduce swelling as well as a pain medication. Probably, he will also suggest no stair climbing or jumping on and off furniture while the dog is healing. My feeling is that because Corgis are short, they are more likely to damage a disc by jumping on and off high objects than a dog with "more leg." Corgis are fearless; keep an eye on yours to prevent too much of that kind of jumping. Also, if you are playing Frisbee or throwing a ball, try to keep the activity low enough that the dog is not leaping high and twisting his back. On the whole, if your dog receives adequate exercise and his weight is okay, then he should not be at risk for back problems any more than any other breed.

Progressive Retinal Atrophy (PRA) seems to be familial (occurring among members of the same family) in Corgis as well, so breeders should be vigilant about eye testing. With PRA, the blood vessels of the retina undergo progressive atrophy. The pupil dilates widely even in daylight. At first there is just "night blindness," but gradually, total blindness occurs. There is no cure. The onset of

PRA can be discovered by an eye exam, where smaller blood vessels will be detected, as well as increased reflectivity in the eye. Dogs affected by PRA should not be bred.

Few veterinarians consider hip dysplasia much of a problem in Corgis, although it is still a good idea to check breeding stock to make sure it is not affected.

Hip dysplasia is an abnormal development of the head of the femur, so that it does not fit properly into the socket. It is considered an inherited disease, but there are outside factors that can contribute to its development, such as rapid growth and excessive exercise. The rapid growth component is one of the reasons why veterinarians encourage people to put their young dogs on adult food as soon as possible. The extra protein in puppy foods can cause too rapid growth.

A dog with hip dysplasia may have a "rolling gait," or "bunny hop," moving both hind legs together, instead of in separate strides. Muscle development of the hind quarters may be poor. A dog may also limp with dysplasia, but the real cause of the limping is likely to be from osteoarthritis, which frequently develops in the joints of dysplastic dogs.

Weight problems also are common in Corgis. These dogs are definitely "chow hounds," so you should monitor the amount you feed your dog. Putting food down at specified times rather than leaving it down all day is a good way to make sure they get a measured amount. An overweight Corgi runs the risk of back problems, as well as the increased weight putting more stress on the dog's heart. Do your dog a favor: Carefully measure food and limit treats.

OTHER CONCERNS

Corgis are basically very healthy. Breeder-veterinarian Lucy Jones says that she has never seen a portal shunt in a Corgi, and, while they do carry the gene for midline septal defects such as cleft palate and umbilical hernias, it is recessive. Portal shunt, which is very rare in Corgis, occurs when blood from the intestines, instead of entering the liver to be cleansed of toxins, bypasses the liver and goes directly to the heart, putting toxins back into the blood stream. A small shunt can be operated on and tied off. The problems of a larger shunt can be lessened by a diet high in carbohydrates and low in protein. Symptoms of a portal shunt are observed a couple of hours after a dog eats. He may seem "spacey," may have temporary blindness, or may have seizures. Fortunately, this is not a major concern for Corgi owners.

An umbilical hernia is a failure of the umbilical ring to close. This is a natural opening in the wall of the abdomen where the umbilical cord is attached. If the ring fails to close, surgery may be needed because of the risk of having circulation interfered with or the bowel obstructed because part of the intestines may protrude through the opening.

The palate is the partition between the dog's mouth and nasal cavity. A cleft palate means the bony plates didn't completely close. This affects the puppy's ability to nurse, because the open palate prevents the proper "air lock" for sucking. Also, food can get into the lungs more easily.

There is not much hope that a puppy can survive a cleft palate because of the difficulty in eating, and the change of food in the lungs. Tube feeding would seem to be the only option, and the length of time and amount of food necessary makes this a daunting task.

If a puppy can be nursed through the first three months of life with careful feeding, an operation can be performed to close the palate.

Unlike some dogs, Corgis do not seem to have any particular sensitivity to anesthetic. If you're concerned, though, you might talk to your doctor about using isoflurane for surgery. Thought to be safer for both animals and people, isoflurane is not water-soluble, so it leaves the animal's system faster and leads to faster recovery.

FIRST AID

Corgis are healthy, but as with any dog, you should watch for certain problems. Any problem that persists longer than 24 hours is reason to call your veterinarian. Any problem that worsens over several hours, such as loss of appetite, weakness or fever, also merits a call to the veterinarian. If your dog has a mild case of diarrhea or vomits once or twice, stop all food for a day and give only water. You may want to feed cooked ground meat with rice for a day or two. If you dog has more frequent bouts of vomiting or diarrhea, or if it continues for more than 24 hours, call the veterinarian.

A dog's normal temperature is between 100°F and 102°F, with a heart rate of 80 to 110 beats per minute. If temperature rises to above 104°F or drops below 100°F, call the veterinarian.

If the dog has a cut that is spurting blood, or if the bleeding can't be stopped by pressure, call the veterinarian.

If you suspect poisoning, don't wait! Call the veterinarian to let the office know you're on the way. If this is not possible, call the ASPCA National Animal Poison Control Center, at 800-548-2423. Have your credit card ready—the center charges a $30 consulting fee. Or, you may call 900-680-0000, and the charges will be added to your phone bill.

Occasionally, something worse will happen. Your dog might get in a fight or, in spite of your best efforts, might get loose and get hit by a car. The first thing to do in an emergency is to take your own pulse. Slow down, take a deep breath and think for a moment about what your best course of action should be. All too often, improper handling on the spur of the moment can result in further injury to the dog and possible injury to you.

The second thing to do is fashion a muzzle for the dog. When a dog is hurt and frightened, he is apt to snap blindly at any touch, even yours. A length of gauze, a rope, a lead or half a pair of pantyhose all work as an emergency muzzle. Make a loop in the middle of your gauze or rope with half a knot. Standing behind the dog, slip this over the muzzle. Bring the ends down under the jaw, and make another half knot. Then draw the ends up behind the ears, and tie them with a quick-release knot or a bow. Do *not* use a muzzle on a dog that is having trouble breathing. Simply restrain the dog with a blanket or some other kind of padding that extends beyond the nose several inches. This will not totally eliminate the chance of a bite, but it will help.

The best way to transport an injured animal is on a blanket or a board, especially if any spinal cord injury is suspected. Get help, if possible, and try to shift the dog all at once to the blanket or board. Try to move the animal as little as possible. Although you may feel that calling the doctor's office is wasting time, your call gives staff members the time they need to prepare for the emergency—take the time to call ahead.

Although cuts and lacerations may produce a lot of blood and look messy and bad, they are probably the least of your concerns. In order of importance, first check the airway and your dog's breathing. Then check circulation: Is the dog in shock? Is there significant blood loss? Check neurologic function: Has any head, neck or back injury likely occurred? Check orthopedic function: Are there any broken bones? Finally, check ocular function: Are any significant eye injuries evident?

OTHER INJURIES

Now you can make note of any cuts, vomiting and bloody urine or stools.

With time and practice, you will not panic over minor problems, but will learn when you can wait and when you need to make an emergency visit to the veterinarian. When in doubt, call your veterinarian—the experts can offer the help and reassurance you need. Better to pay for an unnecessary office visit than ignore something and be sorry later.

Ch. Elfwish Jasmine and Ch. Elfwish Gabriel. (Photo by Sandra Wolfskill)

CHAPTER 7

Caring for Your Pembroke Welsh Corgi

Corgis are energetic dogs, but they are not hyperactive. A couple brisk walks or some running around the yard, coupled with a game or two of fetch, takes care of their minimum needs. In terms of exercise, one of the nice things about a Corgi is its size. In inclement weather, you can exercise the dog indoors. Almost all Corgis love to play ball, and a tennis ball is soft enough to be a fairly safe toy indoors. Or, you can start a game of tag and get a little exercise yourself. If you have multiple dogs, especially those close in age, they just may exercise themselves.

Depending on how your house is arranged, you may be able to practice obedience training indoors as well. If you decide to show, herd, track and do agility or obedience work, these activities also will provide additional exercise for your dog.

EXERCISE EQUIPMENT

Brisk walks are good for both you and your dog. Use a buckle or training collar and a 6-foot lead in leather or nylon. Chain leads are not a good idea because if you need to grab the lead itself, the chain being pulled through your hand will make you very uncomfortable. You also can use a retractable lead if

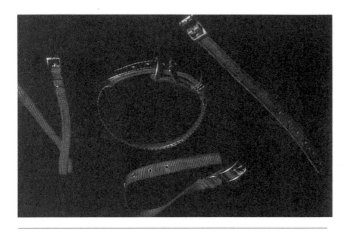

Different types of buckle collars are available. A rolled leather collar is gentler on neck fur; flat leather and nylon are other choices. (Photo by Todd Brininger)

A solid fence is a good idea—a dog probably won't bark at what he can't see. (Photo by Winter/Churchill)

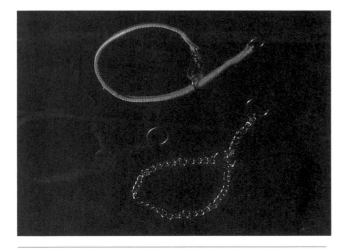

Training collars can be made from chain or nylon. Those made of nylon are less damaging to fur. You can also get a collar with a "free" ring, which enables you to fasten the collar around your dog's neck instead of sliding the collar over his head. (Photo by Todd Brininger)

you have lots of space and want to give your dog some extra freedom. Retractable leads come in 16- and 26-foot lengths, as well as a 32-foot length that is heavier than you would want for an ordinary walk with your Corgi. Shorten the lead if you are walking among other people or dogs. Remember, though, that although retractable leads are a great invention, when the person at one end of the lead is inattentive, the dog can become a nuisance or get into serious trouble.

If you have a fenced yard, you don't need enforced walks, but a single dog will not necessarily exercise itself. A single dog usually needs another dog, or you, to get it moving. If you have an overhead line for a run or are tying the dog out (*not* all day, of course!), make sure to use a buckle collar. *Never* use a training or choke collar on your dog if you are not with the dog. Also, never tie out the dog or even let it run in the yard wearing such a collar—it is all too easy for the slip ring to catch on something, and your dog can choke to death very quickly. If two dogs are playing together, their collars can get caught. A training collar is just that—a collar for training. It should never be left on your dog, indoors or out, if you are not actually training. Attach the dog's tags to a buckle collar, and put that on your dog when you are not there.

Two dogs also will play together and give each other exercise. (Photo by Susan Ewing)

A fenced yard is ideal because you can pop the dogs in and out without much thought. It's particularly useful if a repairman is at the front door and the Corgis can be ushered out the back! While some Corgis climb, most don't need a high fence—3 feet would probably be sufficient, although I'd feel better at 4 feet. In fact, my fence is 5 feet because a friend reminded me that, at 4 feet, other dogs could jump in! Corgis will dig as puppies, but they do not have the terrier urge to *really* dig, so you shouldn't need to bury part of your fence or build a base of concrete. If your neighbors are close, though, consider a stockade fence or some other solid fence. What your dog can't see, he probably won't bark at.

Invisible fencing is also an option. This fence actually consists of a wire buried around the perimeter of your yard. The dog wears a special collar, which activates a warning sound as he approaches the hidden wire. If the dog continues toward the wire, he receives a mild shock. The installer should help you train your dog, or you should find another installer. You don't just install the fence and then collar the dog—the dog needs to understand and know what to expect. Some training is necessary.

Remember, though, that although an invisible fence keeps your dog in, it doesn't keep other dogs out. Our male Corgis would never hesitate to meet an intruder head on, no matter how much bigger the other dog was, and that could mean disaster for a Corgi. I also like to supervise dog/child contact in neighborhoods with small children, and that's easier with a "real" fence.

No matter what kind of fence, run, or tie-out you use, do not leave your dog outdoors when you are not home. Too much can happen. For one thing, dog-nappers are out there. Or, if you use a tie-out, the dog could get tangled or spill its water and be left thirsty. Shade shifts as well—while you

Three dogs together are even more fun! (Photo by Kathryn Smith)

A stroll through autumn leaves is a pleasant way to exercise. (Photo by Lucy E. Jones, DVM)

Dogs always enjoy playtime with their humans. (Photo by Winter/Churchill)

are away, will your dog be in full sun with no escape? Will the dog bark at everything and become a nuisance? Be responsible. Protect your dog and be considerate of your neighbors.

In spite of all your care, your dog might someday wiggle out the unguarded door, find a hole in the fence and get loose. That's why all dogs should have a buckle collar with the tags attached. A rolled leather collar lessens coat damage if you are showing the dog. Tattoos are another good way to permanently identify your dog, or you could have a microchip implanted between the dog's shoulder blades. These microchips can be read by a scanner,

This Corgi enjoys a solitary ballgame, safe inside his fenced yard. (Photo by Winter/Churchill)

which most shelters and veterinarians' offices now have. The chip number is registered, and the dog owner can then be contacted if the dog is found.

TOYS

A dog might play by himself if there's water involved! (Photo by Susan Ewing)

My Corgis love toys, but squeaky ones don't last too long—my male especially can chew out the squeaky part in about 30 to 45 seconds. Latex toys are fine for puppies, but as they get older, a Corgi is able to destroy one very quickly. Pieces of latex will pass harmlessly through your dog, but you should throw away the hard plastic part that makes the squeak if it gets chewed loose. Because latex is so destructible, I lean toward hard rubber toys, nylon bones and a few real bones. If my dogs receive a stuffed toy, I supervise Griffin for the half-hour or so that it takes him to disembowel the toy, and then I remove the squeaky, pull out all the stuffing and let the dogs have the plush part to carry around. They may gnaw on it a bit, but once

Puppies need toys to chase and chew—and hide behind when it's time for a nap. (Photo by Lucy E. Jones, DVM)

Playing tug-of-war with a dominant dog is not a good idea. (Photo by Winter/Churchill)

This lucky Corgi is well equipped with an ID tag, a collar and leash, a bowl and lots of toys. (Photo by Winter/Churchill)

it no longer squeaks, they seem to lose interest in chewing really hard. If they do settle down for a good gnaw, I replace the plush with a bone or a ball, or I distract them with a game.

Puppies need something to chew on when they are teething (usually at age 3 to 6 months old), and they find chair legs just dandy. If you value your furniture, make sure that puppies have toys to chew. A knotted sock will work, as will raw carrots, but if there are adult dogs around, the carrots won't last long.

Rawhide bones are only an occasional treat when I have the time to supervise, because with multiple dogs the rawhide seems to cause more arguments than the other bones and toys. Rawhide is a good way to keep their teeth clean, though, so it's not a bad idea to try to add it to the toy mix.

Corgis enjoy chasing Frisbees, too, but be careful how high you toss the toy—just because Corgis are short doesn't mean that the dog won't twist and leap after the disk, and that can lead to a back injury.

Use caution when playing tug-of-war with a dog. My males have always been too eager to be dominant, and I have not wanted to encourage any aggression or risk losing to them—it's hard enough being the leader of the pack in the family without that! Some Corgis may be fine with this, though, so try to figure out what works for your own dog. For safety reasons, I don't recommend games in which a dog uses its mouth, yet I had one Corgi that played with her mouth all the time and never crossed the line between playful mouthing and a bite.

GOOD NUTRITION

Nutrition is a tricky subject—and there would be only one dog food on the market if it weren't. My basic advice is this: Listen to your breeder and listen to your dog. It's fine to pick a great brand-name puppy food that everyone recommends, but if it's too rich and your puppy throws up or has diarrhea, then it isn't the right food for you, no matter what its reputation.

When I was raising puppies, I had all four on a premium puppy food. Three of the four loved it and did well. The fourth couldn't handle it; it was too rich.

Because I owned a large dog when I got my first Corgi, I got into the habit of feeding twice a day, as a way to prevent bloat in the large dog. Bloat, or gastric torsion, can occur if a dog eats rapidly before or after strenuous exercise or, sometimes, just from eating rapidly. Gasses swell the stomach and in extreme cases, the stomach flips over, or turns on itself, sealing off the opening from the esophagus and to the intestine. If not detected in time, this can be fatal. A Corgi is not prone to bloat, so breaking up meals is not as big an issue

with them, but I still like feeding them twice a day. Of course, puppies will eat three times a day until they are 6 months old, and all my dogs get a good night biscuit as they settle into their crates.

Many people feel that all-natural meals are best, and certainly I have read books that carefully list the proper quantities of meat, vegetables and vitamins that make up a balanced diet. This is not a project for the faint of heart—feeding an all-natural diet takes dedication, time and care. It is not a question of just throwing some ground meat in the bowl and adding some leftover vegetables—you need to provide a well-balanced diet. If you decide that you want to cook for your dog, study carefully and make sure that you have the time to be consistent and to do it right. Otherwise, ask for advice from other owners, study the list of ingredients and select a quality prepackaged food that will meet your dog's nutritional needs.

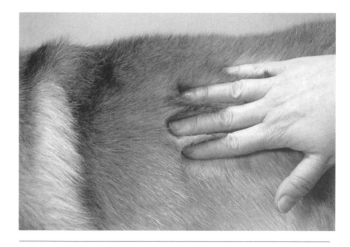

You should be able to feel the dog's ribs, but not be able to count them. (Photo by Winter/Churchill)

I prefer dry foods that help clean a dog's teeth and provide something to chew. (Well, our bitches seem to chew; our male just puts his muzzle in and inhales.) Semi-moist foods have more sugar and coloring in them than I am comfortable with feeding. Many canned foods are excellent as well, but they usually are more expensive to feed than dry food, and, again, don't provide the opportunity to chew.

I have found several brands of dog food that are fine for the Corgis. However, Griffin is allergic to corn, which is in almost all dog foods, so I went through a lot of different kinds before I found a chicken-and-rice food that has no corn. Food allergies are fairly common in dogs and some dogs react more strongly than others. In *The Holistic*

A happy, healthy pet is possible only with a good diet, adequate exercise, proper grooming and lots of love. (Photo by Gail Painter)

Guide for a Healthy Dog by Wendy Volhard and Kerry Brown, DVM, the authors suggest that reactions to some grains are ethnic. Many dogs developed and imported from Europe tend to be allergic to corn, which, until recently, was not a grain fed to dogs in Europe. If your dog has itchy skin and/or by running eyes, and the itchy skin doesn't seem to have any external cause, like fleas, it may be allergic to some part of the food it is eating. You can experiment on your own, or test for food allergies by buying special food from your veterinarian. Frequently, a food to test for allergies is made up of just one ingredient, such as duck or venison. Then, gradually, other ingredients are added. Steroids may offer some relief to itching skin, but it is not a cure; it just relieves a symptom.

Adult Corgis vary in how much food they need. I have seen adults do well eating from one cup a day to $1^{3}/_{4}$ cups. One of my puppies was eating $1^{3}/_{4}$ cups a day but now as a young adult, is fine with $1^{1}/_{4}$ cups; our oldest bitch got 1 cup, and our male was eating $1^{1}/_{2}$ cups and still looking lean. After neutering, he is eating 1 cup, however, and I really have to watch extra biscuits and treats to keep him from getting that pudgy look.

Corgis are hearty eaters when they have the chance. If your Corgi goes off his food, suspect a problem. Also monitor the amount your Corgi eats, because these dogs easily can become "chow hounds." An occasional pizza crust never hurt anybody, but don't overdo the snacks. Check your dog's ribs routinely—you should be able to feel the ribs. If you can't, it's time for a doggy diet. Conversely, if you can *count* the ribs, it's time to increase what you feed.

While snacks—especially "people food" snacks—should be limited, two foods should never be fed. Chocolate is deadly (especially dark chocolate or baker's chocolate), so be extra careful about leaving chocolate where a Corgi can get it. Too much can be fatal. Remember that a table is not necessarily a safe place—a chair nearby could provide a handy step. The other food to avoid is onion, which is probably easier, because there are not usually bowls of onions on side tables. Onion can cause hemolytic anemia, so don't give onions even if your dogs beg. Hemolytic anemia is very rare but, as mentioned, can be caused by a dog eating onions. Symptoms include pale mucus membranes, loss of energy and lack of appetite. A dog may also feel the cold more than usual and seek warm places. The dog may run a fever, and the heart rate may increase. Treatment may include a transfusion and/or vitamin B-12.

This Corgi is anxious for summertime and backyard barbecues. He won't share the human food, but he'll certainly share the fun! (Photo by Kathryn Smith)

Vitamin Supplements

Many veterinarians will tell you never to give vitamin supplements because this can throw off the balance found in dog foods. Many dog breeders, however, will recommend various supplements. I give kelp in winter because it helps keep the dogs' noses black. I also give vitamin C because it reportedly helps them process stress; if the dogs are being shown or are boarded, I like to think that the vitamin helps them. Vitamin C also is a water-soluble vitamin—it doesn't build up in the tissues, but instead it gets flushed out of the system.

My puppies get a little yogurt or cottage cheese for a little extra calcium. Also, both are good products for hiding pills when needed. A bit of cooked egg now and then is also acceptable—be sure to cook it for the same reason that you cook your own eggs: to eliminate the danger of salmonella.

Multi-vitamin tablets also are on the market, as are lots of additives for a healthy coat. They don't seem to do any harm, although whether they do any good will depend on whom you talk to. Again, talk to your breeder and your veterinarian.

With proper exercise, a few well-chosen toys, and a balanced diet, your Corgi should be with you a long time. That's not a bad investment for the return: all that love.

Ch. Belroyd Seabird, ROMX. (Photo by Perry Phillips)

CHAPTER 8

Grooming Your Pembroke Welsh Corgi

Corgis are wash-and-wear dogs, which is one of their attractions as a family pet or as a show or per-formance dog. Their double coat sheds water and dirt, and does not mat or tangle. No regular appointments with the groomer are needed, either—what care the dogs require can be easily done by the owner. This doesn't mean, however, that your dog's grooming can be neglected. Good hygiene is as important to a Corgi's health as it is to a person's health. Corgis also do shed, so regular brushing keeps the number and size of the dust bunnies in your house at a manageable level.

TEETH

Let's start at the front end with the teeth. The care of teeth is an important part of the health of your Corgi. Tartar buildup can lead to abscesses, and bacteria from those abscesses can circulate throughout the system and may cause pneumonia or heart problems. Take action before there is a problem.

There are many products on the market for tooth care, including fingertip bristles and dog tooth-brushes and toothpaste. A piece of gauze wrapped around your finger works, too. Just remember, don't use people toothpaste. If you want to use a paste, buy one especially for dogs.

Giving your dog treated bones or bones made of nylon can help control the tartar, too. Although logic would seem to indicate that dry food is better for teeth, my own veterinarian has seen no difference between dogs on dry food and dogs fed canned food. He recommends such products as nylon bones that dogs actually chew. Most of the time, dogs (at least most Corgis) seem to just inhale their food and don't chew it anyway.

Cleanings by your veterinarian are a good idea, although frequency will vary as some dogs seem more prone to tartar buildup than others. Check your dog's teeth and check with your veterinarian.

A clean, well-groomed Corgi is a happy Corgi. (Photo by Winter/Churchill)

TRIMMING

You don't need to do much trimming on a Corgi, whether your dog is a pet or a show dog. You might want to trim the fur around the feet. You can neaten the fur over the nails, and it's a good idea to trim the fur between the pads, especially during the winter when that hair can trap snow and ice. Some people trim the whiskers on show dogs; some leave their dog *au naturel*. I have done both; although I prefer to leave the whiskers on, trimming them doesn't seem to bother the dog. That's all there is to it—Corgis don't need a lot of fussing.

GENERAL GROOMING

To say that there's not much trimming is not to say that no grooming is necessary, though. All dogs should be groomed to keep them both looking good and feeling good. Regular grooming can help you prevent problems before they start and also can help you find potential problems, such as the start of a hot spot or any unusual bumps or growths. You may also find fleas or ticks that are well-hidden in the dense coat.

Ideally, grooming every day is the best. It makes for very short sessions because shedding and dirt are taken care of immediately. If that's not possible, grooming three times a week can keep a Corgi neat, tidy and ready for a cluster of shows. If you groom just once a week, the session will take a bit longer but will still keep your dog looking good. Missing a week usually will not result in impossible mats or tangles, but you should try for once a week at least.

Equipment

There's not a lot of equipment involved, either. First, get a grooming table, or if you don't care about the ease of one that folds up, make one.

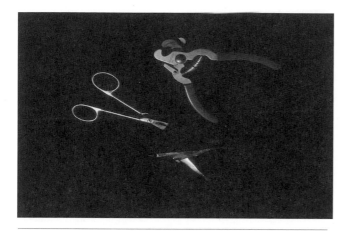

These are three types of nail clippers. At the bottom is a guillotine blade, at the center is a small scissors type and at the top is a larger clipper with blades that squeeze together. (Photo by Todd Brininger)

From left to right, a soft-bristle "finishing" brush, a rubber-toothed shedding rake, a slicker brush and a cat brush all are good grooming tools. (Photo by Todd Brininger)

Nonslip rubber matting is a good choice for the surface. I made do for a while with a piece of floor matting on top of my clothes dryer, but a table is better because you can walk around a table and easily get to all sides of your dog. Corgis are too short to be able to groom them effectively on the ground, as your back will soon tell you. Also, putting the dog up on something makes it easier to control them. A table with a grooming arm enables you to slip the grooming loop over the dog's head, which helps hold the dog in position while you work.

I also recommend using a grooming smock. You probably will be much more apt to groom when you know that you will not end up covered with Corgi hair. If you don't want to buy a smock, designate an old shirt as the "dog shirt." Just choose something that you can easily slip on over whatever you are wearing.

You'll want combs that range from fairly wide-set teeth to very fine teeth. The comb at the top of the picture is a flea comb, which has the most teeth per inch and is a good finishing comb—it's also effective at removing fleas. (Photo by Todd Brininger)

Cotton balls are useful for cleaning ears and, when bathing your dog, you might want to use some cotton in each ear to keep out the water. Cotton balls may also be used around the eyes to gently wipe away any dirt. Baby wipes come in handy for fast removal of dirt and for cleaning ears and feet. You'll also want a slicker brush as well as several combs of varying tooth count. A greyhound comb is a good start with its two sizes, and a flea comb is the finest and has the most number of teeth per inch. A wide-tooth comb grabs undercoat and dirt but doesn't leave a smooth, finished look. Start your grooming with the comb with the widest teeth, then go to one with closer spacing to grab even more undercoat, then move to even closer spacing to finish the job. If you start with the finest comb first, chances are there will be too much coat for the comb to effectively do its job. Of course, the more often you comb and brush your dog, the finer comb you can use. You also might want to use a regular soft-bristle brush. If you're showing and are using powder, chalk, or cornstarch for cleaning feet, a small baby brush or cat

All dogs should be groomed to keep them both looking good and feeling good. (Photo by Winter/Churchill)

brush works well, both for applying the powder and for brushing it out. Shedding combs are available that really go after the dead undercoat when a dog is shedding heavily. I favor one with short, hard rubber teeth—it doesn't seem to hurt the rest of the coat, and it really grabs the undercoat when my dogs are shedding. A hair dryer is nice for use after your dog has a bath, but vigorous toweling will work just as well. Use common sense, and keep the dog in a warm environment until it is dry. Swedish saunas aside, turning your dog loose to romp in the snow after a bath is not a good idea.

If you decide you want to use a hair dryer, buy one especially for dogs. These special dryers blow cool to only slightly warm air. An ordinary human hair dryer usually produces temperatures much too high to use on a dog. If you plan to use a human dryer, make sure it has an extra-low setting. The air should not feel very hot at all on your hand.

Different groomers and breeders have different ideas about the very best grooming tools. The important thing is to have a regular grooming schedule and stick to it.

Doing the Job

Okay, let's say that your dog is on the table. First check your dog's mouth and teeth. At least three times a week, clean the teeth, as discussed. Then check the eyes. Wipe away any crud with a damp cotton ball or a soft cloth. Also check the ears. Corgis don't have many ear problems, but dirt can collect. Use a baby wipe or cotton ball to sweep away dirt. You also can use professional ear-cleaner solution, if you like. Whatever you use, *do not* push into the ear canal! Move out and away as you clean.

Check the hair on the feet, and trim it if needed. You can do the nails while the dog is on the table, but Corgis are notorious for not wanting their feet touched—you might find it easier to hold the Corgi on his back on your lap. (More about this later.) Check the fur around the anal area for any fecal matter as well. Corgis are pretty clean, but it's a good idea to check just in case.

Before you start brushing, mist the dog's coat with water—you want the coat slightly damp to prevent it from breaking. Some people like to add a little conditioner as well. I actually use a little Listerine because it's antiseptic and smells nice. (The definitive word here is *little*—you want water, not additive.) Depending on whether the dog is shedding or "blowing coat," first go over the dog with the shedding rake. If you've been grooming regularly, you can probably skip this step and start with your slicker brush. Start at the rear of the dog and work on small areas at a time. With one hand, hold back the fur against the grain. Start at the base of that bit of hair, and brush it back into

You should teach your dog to allow you to handle his feet as well as to trim his nails. (Photo by Winter/Churchill)

place, away from your hand. Continue, cleaning the brush frequently. Keep doing this as long as you are getting hair, paying special attention to the hindquarters, which always seem to be thickest. Then switch to a comb. It's amazing how much more hair you can get with a down-to-the-skin combing. Switch to a comb with finer teeth, if needed. Finish with a quick once-over with the soft bristle brush, and reward with a treat.

Anyone you ever talk to about dogs will tell you that if you begin clipping nails while a puppy is young, your dog will get used to your handling his feet. My experience with Corgis says that the first half of that sentence is true. You should indeed start young. Whether or not the dog gets used to it, however, is a different question entirely. Our male still appears convinced that his toes will be amputated and that he should avoid this situation at all cost. When he's actually having it done, he must yelp at least once as though he's being tortured. This yelp may or may not coincide with a nail actually being clipped.

What seems to work well with a Corgi is holding the dog on your lap instead of putting him on a table. This means that the dog's head is just to the left or right of your chin, and its back runs down across your chest, with the rump in your lap. Using a grinder or clippers, proceed to cut the nails. Cutting right about where the nail curls should assure a cut that will miss the quick. If you do hit the quick, just apply some styptic powder to stop the

Some pups don't mind baths much . . .

. . . while others require extra help to keep them in the tub. (Photos by Winter/Churchill)

bleeding, or apply pressure until the bleeding stops. Grinding takes off less nail at a time than clippers do, but Corgis seem to find a grinder less offensive, and it leaves a nice finished look.

You'll find many bathing products on the market, and you'll find just about as many opinions about bathing. Your own dog's activity level will help dictate how frequent baths should be. Besides spot cleaning (or bathing if the dog gets really dirty), I bathe my dogs two or three days before a show. A bath tends to fluff up the coat and make it a bit less manageable, so I want the coat to have those two or three days to return to a normal look. At the actual show, I clean the feet with a powder-cornstarch mixture, and then brush and comb the coat. Winter baths are less frequent, both because of the cold and because too many baths can dry the coat and skin.

A bath when the dog is shedding helps loosen the hair and speed the shedding process. Sometimes just some spot cleaning with dry or waterless shampoo is all that's needed. Our oldest bitch's coat and skin have changed with age, and she needs more frequent baths than the younger dogs do. Ask your veterinarian, ask your breeder, ask your friends and pay attention to each individual dog. One size does not fit all when it comes to baths.

And that's it for grooming your Corgi. With a little brushing and an occasional bath, you won't mind a bit if your dog shares your bed.

Ch. Elfwish Lyleth. (Photo by Ashbey Photography)

CHAPTER 9

Showing Your Pembroke Welsh Corgi

Maybe you purchased your puppy specifically for show, or maybe you got the idea later when the breeder or friends made the suggestion. However you thought of it, it's a great way to be with your dog and have fun. Most all-breed clubs have both conformation and obedience divisions at their shows, and many are now adding agility competition. (Don't worry if your dog is not show-quality; there are lots of other fun things you can do. This chapter just happens to be about showing your dog in conformation shows.)

GETTING STARTED

Conformation shows grew out of livestock judging, and their purpose is to find the dogs that are the closest to their breed standard and, thus, that are the best breeding stock. For this reason, dogs competing in conformation may not be spayed or neutered.

There are no disqualifications in the Pembroke Welsh Corgi standard, but there are serious faults. If your Corgi has one of these, it would be best to spay or neuter the dog and enjoy other events. Serious faults include fluffies, mismarks and bluies in coat and coloring. Incorrect ear set is also a serious fault.

Read the standard carefully (see Chapter 3, "Official Standard of the Pembroke Welsh Corgi"). If your dog has no serious faults and someone whose opinion you value says that the dog is show quality, then give showing a try.

Equipment

Besides your dog, you'll need a show collar and a lead. These are lighter in weight than what you would use for a walk in the park, and a show lead also might be shorter. Ask your breeder or other handlers for recommendations. Most Corgis are shown on a light training collar and lead, but some handlers use the all-in-one leads. This is a matter of personal choice: Use what you're comfortable with and what gives you the best control of your dog.

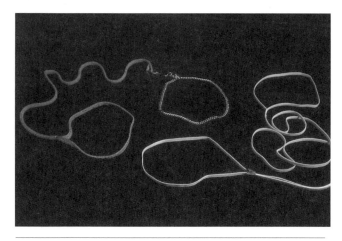

These are two lead choices for showing. On the left is a short, soft lead with a lightweight training collar. On the right is an all-in-one lead that features a metal slide to adjust the loop that goes over the dog's head. (Photo by Todd Brininger)

Corgis tend to put their head down to check out all the great smells, so a light training collar may give you more control and help keep the dog's head up.

If your local club offers handling classes, this provides an excellent place to learn, to practice and to get your dog used to other people and dogs. At class, you'll practice "gaiting" your dog—moving the dog at a trot, counterclockwise around the ring with the other handlers and dogs. The judge will also ask to see your dog moved individually. Usually judges request a simple "down and back," or a triangle, although they may ask for an L-shaped pattern as well. Practice all these so that you're comfortable with them and can move your dog at the best pace to show him off. No dog is perfect, and your dog may look better at a slower rather than faster pace, or vice versa. Ask other class members what they think. If there's a mirror where you practice, watch your dog as you move at different speeds.

Corgis are examined on a table, so you'll need to get your dog used to that, too. Start your puppy young, and keep sessions short and happy. Put the puppy on the table, and encourage him to stretch forward for a treat. Position the puppy to show off his silhouette to the best advantage—this is called "stacking." Check his teeth, as the judge will do. Using treats is a good way to tell the puppy that a hand approaching means something yummy, not something to be feared or avoided. Handle the puppy's feet and, if you have a male, check the testicles. The judge will, so this shouldn't come as a surprise to your dog in the show.

The Pembroke Welsh Corgi (above) is a sturdy, independent and bold breed. Although Corgis appear to be small dogs (top right), it's more appropriate to think of them as short-legged big dogs. This Corgi (lower right) is the apple of someone's eye. Corgis are sociable dogs and like to be with their people. (Photos by Winter/Churchill)

Bred to herd cattle and geese, Corgis love to be outside in any weather (top). They shouldn't live outdoors, however. (Photo by Lucy E. Jones, DVM) Corgis have a weatherproof double coat (bottom left). A softer, finer coat underlies a coarser, heavier outer coat. (Photo by Winter/Churchill) A Corgi puppy makes a new friend (bottom right). Corgis are great household pets, even in small quarters. (Photo by Irma Hilts)

Although Corgis are short, they think that they are big dogs. Corgis can be fearless and strong-willed, but they take well to training. (Photo by Gail Painter)

These Corgis (top) demonstrate some of the color variations in the breed. The two on the outside have different shadings of red and flank the tricolor in the middle. A Corgi (left) looks inquisitively into the camera. Corgis are noted for their intelligent expression. (Photos by Gail Painter)

Corgis love to be part of the action. They are quick learners and excel at obedience, agility, tracking and herding competitions (above) and like to play games around the house (below). (Photo above by Tien Tran Photography; photo right by Winter/Churchill)

Corgis are energetic dogs, so good hygiene, such as occasional baths (left), and plenty of exercise (top) are vital to keeping them happy and healthy. (Photos by Winter/Churchill)

Two Corgis patiently wait to reenter a house (top). Although well-equipped for the outdoors, Corgis enjoy indoor comforts. A correct Corgi is low-set, strong and sturdily built (bottom right). Corgi puppies have individual personalities. A dedicated breeder will help you select the right puppy for your household (bottom left). (Photos by Winter/Churchill)

The Pembroke Welsh Corgi is a terrific companion, ready to join you on any adventure. (Photo by Winter/Churchill)

Your dog will quickly figure out that when the show lead goes on, it's time to have fun! (Photo by Winter/Churchill)

Start training your puppy early on if you plan to show him later. Keep your lessons short and happy. (Photo by Maxine Ellis)

Offer whatever bait your dog likes. This beauty is Ch. Sandyshire's The Phantom (Am./Can. Ch. Blaizewood Hooray Henry ex Sandyshire's Seamist). (Photo by K9's in Motion)

You'll also want your dog to "free bait" for you. This means that the dog stands squarely so that the judge can get a good look. Offer whatever bait your dog likes. Liver is a standard form of bait, but many people use cheese, chicken or even left-over steak. However, what your dog will respond to in class, he may ignore under the increased pressure of a real show, so experiment. One handler I know used raisins in the ring!

An outdoor show: The Best of Breed class at the 1999 PWCCA National Specialty involved 88 beautiful Corgis! (Photo by Susan Ewing)

These Corgis are in the ring at an outdoor all-breed dog show. (Photo by Douglas Nickels)

If liver is your bait of choice, here are two ways to fix it. First, rinse the liver in cold water, then put in a pan with cold water and bring to a boil. Boil 20 minutes. Remove the liver from the pan and place on a cookie sheet. Sprinkle with garlic powder. Bake 20 to 30 minutes at 300 degrees. Place in plastic bags or wrap in foil and freeze for use when needed.

Or, you may place the liver on a layer of paper towels, cover with paper towels and microwave for three minutes on high; turn the pieces, and microwave for another three minutes. Freeze as mentioned.

Whether you're practicing on your own or at a class—and you should be doing both—keep lessons short and fun.

The Prep Work

When you feel ready to show, consider attending matches first for practice. Matches are run along the same lines as shows, but no points are awarded and the entry fees are lower. Currently, it costs close to $20 to enter a point show, although many clubs do give a discount to puppy entries. Match entry fees are around $5.

There are two types of conformation shows: benched and unbenched. The majority of shows today are unbenched. At a benched show, dogs are grouped together by breed in a central area and are on display during the entire show, except for grooming, exercising and showing. At an unbenched show, you may keep your dog anywhere when not showing, and you are not

❏ **MASTER** or ❏ **VISA**   FOR FAX ENTRY ONLY - FEE $4 PER ENTRY   **EXPIRATION DATE**
CARD NO.

CARD HOLDER
NAME

SHOW		DATE

I ENCLOSE $_____ for entry fees.
IMPORTANT - Read Carefully Instructions on Reverse Side Before Filling Out. Numbers in the boxes
indicate sections of the instructions relevant to the information needed in that box. (PLEASE PRINT)

BREED	VARIETY (1)	SEX

	DOG (2) (3) SHOW CLASS	CLASS (3) DIVISION Weight, Color, etc.	
	ADDITIONAL CLASSES	OBEDIENCE TRIAL CLASS	JR. SHOWMANSHIP CLASS

NAME OF (See Back)
JUNIOR HANDLER (if any)

FULL NAME
OF
DOG

❏ AKC REG. NO.   Enter number here | DATE OF BIRTH
❏ AKC LITTER NO.
❏ ILP NO.   PLACE OF ❏ USA ❏ CANADA ❏ FOREIGN
❏ FOREIGN REG NO. & COUNTRY   BIRTH   Do not print the above in catalog

BREEDER

SIRE

DAM

ACTUAL   Please Check If
OWNER(S)
(4)   (Please Print)   ❏ OWNERSHIP CHANGE
OWNER'S   or
ADDRESS   ❏ ADDRESS CHANGE

CITY   STATE   ZIP

NAME OF OWNER'S AGENT
(IF ANY) AT THE SHOW   ID #

I CERTIFY that I am the actual owner of the dog, or that I am the duly authorized agent of the actual owner whose name I have entered above. In consideration of the acceptance of this entry, I (we) agree to abide by the rules and regulations of The American Kennel Club in effect at the time of this show or obedience trial, and by any additional rules and regulations appearing in the premium list for this show or obedience trial or both, and further agree to be bound by the Agreement printed on the reverse side of this entry form. I (we) certify and represent that the dog entered is not a hazard to persons or other dogs. This entry is submitted for acceptance on the foregoing representation and agreement.

SIGNATURE of owner or his agent
duly authorized to make this entry

Telephone   Pers. ID Code #

This is a copy of a dog show entry form.

required to stay for the rest of the show after you show your dog. Dog shows of any type can be held outdoors, with or without tents, or indoors.

Shows are also either all-breed or specialty shows. An all-breed show is just what it sounds like—it is open to all AKC-registered breeds. A specialty show is a show for one breed of dog, and local, regional or national breed-specific clubs sponsor these shows. Sometimes a local club for a specific breed will consider its entry at an all-breed show as a specialty show. If that is the case, the club usually will have its own trophy table and probably will add nonregular classes, such as Sweepstakes and Veterans, to the judging.

Shows are managed by superintendents, companies set up to handle putting on a show. Typically, superintendents send out premium lists, take entries, mail out judging schedules, supply the ribbons or rosettes, supply judges' books, have catalogs printed, record wins and set up and tear down rings. For indoor shows, they supply and install the rubber matting in the rings. At outdoor shows, they do not usually provide tenting; the presenting club makes those arrangements. Local club members also are responsible for cleanup, parking, vendors and any transportation and hospitality for judges.

You can find the names and addresses of licensed superintendents in the front of the events section of the *AKC Gazette*. (You do get the *Gazette*, don't you? See Appendix A, "Resources," for details.) Call or write, and ask to be added to the superintendents' mailing lists. That way, you

will get premium lists sent to you. A premium list contains entry forms that are returned to the superintendent along with the listed entry fee. The premium list also tells you the presenting club, the location of the show, whether the show is indoors or out, who the judges are, and whether any trophies are offered for your breed. The premium list usually includes directions to the show site and will tell you if any particular breed will not be entered. (Specialty shows may not be held unless all-breed shows held at the same time within a radius of 200 miles agree that they will not accept entries from that breed.)

The entry form has a place for your name, the breeder's name, the dog's registered name, the AKC registration number, the dog's sex, the dog's date of birth and what class you plan to enter.

SHOW CATEGORIES

Class choices are Puppy 6–9 Months, Puppy 9–12 Months, 12–18 Months, Novice, American-Bred, Bred-by-Exhibitor and Open. Entrants in the Novice class may not have any points, may not have won more than three first places from the Novice class, or may not have won a first place in any other class except a Puppy class. The American-Bred class requires the dog to have been bred in the United States. In the Bred-by-Exhibitor class, the owner or co-owner must have bred the dog, or must be a member of the immediate family. Any dog may be entered in the Open class.

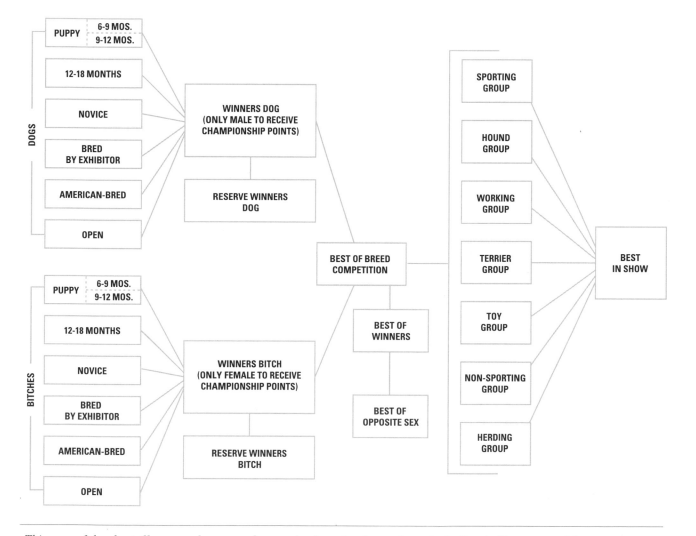

This copy of the chart illustrates the way a show works, from the classes through the Best in Show competition.

Classes are divided, with dogs competing against dogs and bitches competing against bitches. Ribbons are awarded for first through fourth place. The first-place winners from each class then compete for Winners Dog or Winners Bitch. These winners are awarded from one to five points toward a championship. To win three, four or five points is to get what is called a major. A championship then is achieved with a total of not less than 15 points, of which the dog must win two majors under two separate judges. The number of points is determined by the number of dogs of the same sex that the dog beat that day. Then, the Winners Dog and the Winners Bitch go back into the ring with any Champions entered to compete for the Best of Breed award. If either of the winners wins Best of Breed or Best of Winners, they may also win more points. For example, there could be enough dogs entered to give the Winners Dog three points, but only enough bitches to win two points. If the bitch beats the dog for Best of Winners, she would get the same number of points that the dog won—in this example, three.

Am./Can. Ch. Lorjen Blaidd Ted E. Brite (Am./Can. Ch. Malvern's Bright and Shiny ex Ch. Blaidd Amanda Cross) is handled here by Roger Ellis. (Photo by Kurtis Photography)

The Best of Breed dog/bitch then goes on to the group show. Corgis are in Group VII, Herding. The seven group winners are then judged for Best in Show.

The point schedule determines how many dogs you must beat for each number of points, and it is broken down into regions. Usually the show catalog will list this for each breed.

The catalog includes the judging schedule and also lists entrants by breed and class. Each entry listing gives the dog's registered name, AKC number, date of birth, owner, breeder and handler, if different. At the back of many catalogs is a list of the names and addresses of the people who have entered. This gives you an easy reference if you like a particular dog and want to contact the owner.

WHAT TO PACK

So now you've got your dog trained, you've cooked your liver as bait, and you've mailed the entry forms. What else is involved? Lots, actually. Packing for a dog show is like packing for a mini-safari. It's hard to believe all the items you'll discover that you just can't do without.

For starters, there's a crate. I prefer an airline crate because it offers more shelter. Also, if someone is inconsiderate enough to let a male dog lift his leg against your crate (and, believe me, someone could possibly be that inconsiderate), a solid side protects both your dog and its bedding. If the show is an indoor show and you are leaving your dog at the site, you'll need only one crate. On the other hand, if you're shuttling your dog back and forth from your motel to the site, you may need one or two more: one crate for the room, and one for the car. I travel with a folding wire crate for the room and a smaller crate for the short rides back and forth between the show site and the motel.

If the dog shares the motel room with you and you permit it on the bed, travel with an old sheet to protect the bedspread. Dog hairs on the rug may be vacuumed, but bedspreads usually need special cleaning. All too many motels are closing their doors to dogs, so help make a good impression. Also, carry lots of plastic bags. There is no excuse for not picking up after your dog—no one else wants to, and there is no reason why they should. Don't give all dog people a bad name; pick up after your dog!

Other items you'll need include bedding for however many crates you have, water and food bowls and both water and food. Taking water from home is a good idea so that you don't risk digestive upsets with strange water. Also pack any medication your dog might need, and take a heavier collar and a lead for walking your dog, and/or a wire exercise pen. You can never have too many towels along, either. You'll need one on the grooming table, one for muddy feet, one to dry the dog if it's raining and extra towels to substitute for wet or dirty bedding. You'll also want a grooming table and your grooming supplies along.

Remember that at all shows, but especially any held at state parks, you'll need your dog's rabies certificate as well. It's a good idea to have a copy of your shot record and rabies certificate with you at all times. Just stuff a copy in your tack box.

You'll need to take at least one crate with you to the dog show. (Photo by Winter/Churchill)

And what will you need for yourself? Well, that varies a bit depending on whether the show is indoors or out. Generally, however, you should follow the Scout motto: "Be prepared." Comfortable, flat-heeled shoes are the first thing. Next are clothes appropriate for a dog show. For men, this is slacks and a sport coat and tie. For women, it means a skirt and a jacket or a blouse, or a nice pants suit. Also, if you're a woman, get in the habit of buying dresses and skirts with pockets for bait. Solid colors that contrast with the dog's coat make a good background for showing off your dog. A raincoat is a good idea, too. If you're not sure what the weather's going to do, dress in layers. Think about packing some quick-energy snacks for yourself as well—dog show food frequently runs in the neighborhood of hot dogs and hamburgers, and there may be only coffee for breakfast.

Recently, my mother traveled with me to a site for four days of shows. After watching several people arrive with dogs, crates, tack boxes, suitcases and other assorted bags and bundles, she commented that dog people must really love their hobby because it was hard work loading and unloading. I reported this to a couple of friends later in the day, and both responded immediately. "It's easier than kids," said one. "It's easier than horses," said the other. So, it's all relative. Certainly, a Corgi is easier to get from point A to point B than a horse, and even with as much as you spend on crates, tables and entry fees, it's still cheaper than college.

FINAL GROOMING

Corgis don't require a lot of grooming, but they should look their best in the ring. Keep nails short, keep foot hair neat and trim the whiskers, if you prefer that look. That's all the trimming allowed, but you'll need combs and brushes for a clean, attractive coat, and you'll want to make sure that those white feet really are clean and white, not puddle gray. Use cornstarch, powder, chalk or a combination of all three. Just make sure that it's all brushed out before you go in the ring—foreign substances in the coat are not permitted in the ring. Clean the ears as well, and make sure that the eyes are clear as well; then head for the ring.

PROFESSIONAL HANDLERS

Maybe you've decided that you want your dog to be shown but that you don't have the time and energy, or the skill to do it yourself. Maybe what you want is a professional handler. Professional handlers make their living showing dogs, so they are very skilled. They will know how to groom your dog so that he looks his best, and they will know how to present him to the judge.

Not every handler handles every breed, and some are better with one breed than another, so ask around. Also observe the professionals at work. I have used four different handlers for different reasons. You also may like a particular handler but find your dog does not. Remember, your dog will be traveling and living with this handler, so it's important that the two get along. Watch the handler in the ring, talk to others about him and talk to him personally.

Make sure that you are clear about fees as well. Most handlers charge a fee for showing and then prorate travel expenses. Boarding fees may or may not be included. There is usually an additional charge if your dog is shown in the group ring and another if it makes it to Best in Show judging. The handling fee for showing your dog at a specialty is frequently double the fee for an all-breed show. Weighed against travel expenses of your own, and with the odds in favor of a professional finishing your dog's championship faster than you could, paying a professional may still be cheaper than doing it yourself.

Whatever approach you take, try to remember that this is supposed to be fun!

Roganway Scallawag, OA, owned by Gwen Platt and Pam Smith. (Photo by Tien Tran)

CHAPTER 10

The Working Pembroke Welsh Corgi

One of the most wonderful things about owning a Corgi is that these dogs can do almost anything you want them to do. You can have terrific fun with a Corgi because the dogs are hardy and can learn just about anything that you can teach them. Obedience, conformation, agility, tracking, herding, therapy, service training—Corgis excel in all these areas. I even had a Siberian Husky breeder tell me that she thought Corgis would have great pulling power. Of course, she added, you lose something in the stride.

OBEDIENCE TRAINING

No matter what you want to do with your Corgi, basic obedience is a good place to start. Whether you are interested in competing or not, every Corgi needs some training. Remember that the dogs are very willing to rule, so be firm and consistent, and teach them some manners. Teach them to come, sit, stay, drop items that you would prefer they didn't have (dead chipmunks come to mind) and get off beds or chairs that you would prefer they weren't on. Teaching them to go to a specific spot, whether it's a crate, a bed or just a designated corner of the room, also may be useful. Formal heeling may not be necessary,

Corgis learn quickly—whether they'll actually do what they've learned is another question entirely. (Drawing by Pat Rapple/Funny Bones)

but walking quietly on a loose lead will make walks much more pleasant as well.

You can train your dog by yourself with the guidance of one or more of the excellent training books on the market. I prefer a class, however, because it motivates me. I make sure that I practice between classes because the instructor and the other pupils will know if I don't. Also, if you're a first-time owner and trainer, it's good to have an experienced person for guidance. If you decide to take a class, shop around first. Not all training methods work with all dogs, even when they are the same breed. Also, if you don't like the

instructor, for whatever reason, you probably won't get all you could from the class. Talk to other dog people, and contact your local all-breed club. Boarding kennels frequently offer classes, as do local recreation centers and YMCAs and YWCAs. Observe a class. If you feel comfortable with the teaching methods, and if the dogs seem happy, sign up.

Besides your dog, you'll need a 6-foot lead (leather, not a chain) and a training collar or a flat, buckle collar. Contrary to some people's beliefs, the training, or choke, collar is not an instrument of torture. It is a training collar, designed to deliver a mild but instant correction during training. The training collar is *not* designed to be worn at all times, especially if the dog is unattended. The loose end can all too easily catch on something, and then it is indeed a choke collar and can lead to death.

If you decide on a metal link training collar, as opposed to a nylon one, check out the smoothness of the links first. Each link should be smooth, with no sharp metal burrs. A collar that has rough links will be more apt to tear and cut the fur around your dog's neck, and also the collar will not slide and release as it should, which lessens its effectiveness.

Obedience instructors used to frown on training with treats ("You can't use them in the ring, so why use them to train?"), but that attitude seems

This Corgi is ready to head for obedience class, or maybe just some practice with her owner. (Photo by Winter/Churchill)

Most people who train Corgis agree that treats, praise and affection are more effective with a recalcitrant Corgi than using harsh corrections. (Photo by Winter/Churchill)

to have disappeared. Treats can be a wonderful motivation—they work well with Corgis, who seem to be very food-oriented, so you'll probably want to carry a pocketful of treats. Of course, lots of praise is essential whether you use food rewards or not, and the best trainers will tell you that you never correct a dog until you are certain that the dog knows what you want. Most people who train Corgis also will tell you that treats, praise and patience are more effective than harsh corrections. That's not to say that you should never correct a dog, but Corgis become offended by such treatment. You are better off with a source of unending patience—and a good sense of humor.

Corgis learn quickly, but then they may start to get creative. If they are bored, they may think of a new way to respond to a command. They may go directly to the "heel" position on recall, instead of stopping to sit in front of you. In an advanced exercise, such as the "drop on recall," they may

decide to crawl toward you to get a head start on the return. Or, they may just decide to sit quietly and watch *you* do the heeling pattern by yourself. It's up to you to think of creative ways to make training interesting and fun.

The Canine Good Citizen Test

Let's say that you've done the basics and are hooked on training. What then? The first step

This fluffy Corgi, Sherman, practices a long sit with his classmates during his obedience class. (Photo by Irma Hilts)

might be to find a club that administers the Canine Good Citizen test (CGC). This is much less formal than Obedience Trails, but it indicates that your dog is a good citizen.

In the test, strangers will approach your dog; the dog should not object to their approach, nor to being petted—it should sit quietly. The dog also must accept grooming (the tester will brush your dog). The dog must walk on a loose lead and remain under control as you walk through a crowd. The dog also must know the sit, down and stay commands and must come when called. The dog will be tested as well to see if it remains calm around another dog and if it reacts calmly to noises, sudden movements and other distractions. Finally, you will be asked to leave your dog; he should not whine, cry or make too much effort to follow.

Formal Obedience Trials

If you really enjoy obedience training and want to compete in formal Obedience Trials, write to the AKC for regulations regarding obedience competition. And, as the violinist was told when he asked how to get to Carnegie Hall, practice, practice, practice.

If you have been working alone but are seriously considering pursuing a Companion Dog (CD) title, it's a good idea to join a class or find some other people to work with. This will accustom your dog to other people and dogs and will get him comfortable with other dogs in proximity for the sits and downs.

To get a CD title on your dog, your dog must earn a score of 170 or better out of a possible 200, and must earn at least 50 percent of the allowable points in each exercise. He will need to do this three times to earn the title. For a CD, the exercises are heel on lead and figure eight, 40 points; stand for examination, 30 points; heel off-lead, 40 points; recall, 30 points; and the long sit (for one minute) and the long down (for three minutes), both 30 points.

After your dog has earned his CD, he can try for a Companion Dog Excellent (CDX) title. Again, he will need to qualify under three different judges and must earn at least 50 percent of allowable points in each category. Exercises in the Open classes are heel free and figure eight, 40 points; drop on recall, 30 points; retrieve on flat, 20 points; retrieve over high jump, 30 points; broad jump, 20 points; long sit, 30 points; and long down, 30 points. In the Open classes, the long sit is for three minutes, and the handlers are taken out of the ring and out of sight. The long down is for five minutes, again with the handlers out of sight.

The broad jump is twice as wide as the high jump, and currently, Corgis jump the height of the dog at the withers, to the nearest 2 inches, as jumps are raised in 2-inch increments. If your Corgi is 12 inches high, he will jump 12 inches for the high jump, and 24 inches for the broad jump. If he is 10 inches high, he will jump 10 and 20 inches; but if he is 11 inches at the withers, he will jump 12 and 24 inches.

The next step in the obedience progression is the Utility Dog (UD) title. Again, the dog will need to appear before three different judges and earn a maximum score of 200, with 50 percent of each exercise. Exercises are the signal exercise (you direct your dog to sit, go down, and come with hand signals), 40 points; scent discrimination (your dog selects one metal and one leather article that has your scent on it), 30 points for each; directed retrieve (the dog retrieves one of three gloves at your direction), 30 points; moving stand and examination, 30 points; and directed retrieve (you direct your dog over either the bar jump or the high jump), 30 points.

If you have gotten this far, you are seriously committed to the sport of obedience and may be thinking of working your dog toward an Obedience championship (OTCH). To earn an

Brookshire Royal Flush, OA ("Thomas") clears a jump easily. (Photo by Carla DeDominicis)

OTCH title, a dog must have a UD title and must have won 100 points in competition, including earning a first place in a Utility class with at least three dogs in the class, earning a first place in the Open B class with at least six dogs in the class and earning a third first place in either of the previous situations. The three first places also must be under three different judges. Points are earned much as they are in conformation, with more points awarded as more dogs are beaten.

AGILITY TRAINING

Agility is becoming a very popular sport because it provides lots of fun and exercise for both the handler and the dog. It is also a very new sport, so the rules and regulations are still being revised. If you are interested in agility competition, there are three major organizations for the sport: the AKC, the United States Dog Agility Association (USDAA) and the North American Dog Agility Council (NADAC). Write to them for the most current regulations (see Appendix A, "Resources").

An example of how things change is that currently the USDAA has a higher A-frame than the other two organizations (6 feet, 3 inches, as opposed to 5 feet, 6 inches), but the organization is just starting a new division called the Performance

Ch. Elfwish Nicholas Nickelby, CD, CAN TD, HC, owned by Lisa Ermer, obviously enjoys his run through the agility course. (Photo by K9's In Motion)

Program, in which the A-frame is lowered to 5 feet, 6 inches. Jumps will also be lowered. How soon this will go into effect is not known, but if you want to compete in all three organizations, this is something to check out.

Each organization has three levels. The AKC has Novice, Open and Excellent levels. The USDAA has Starters/Novice, Advanced and Master levels. The NADAC has Novice, Open and Elite levels. Your dog also can go on to win Agility championships in each organization. With each level, the number

Fluffy "Sherman" learns to walk the dog walk on an agility course. (Photo by Irma Hilts)

Rojanway Fly In Style, NA, breaks from the chute. (Photo by Tien Tran)

Brookshire Royal Flush, OA, known as "Thomas," is owned by Gwen Platt. Besides being a good agility dog, Thomas was in the Disney movie Murder, She Purred. *(Photo by Jerry Roberts)*

A hesitation or a refusal can cost valuable time. (Drawing by Pat Rapple/Funny Bones)

"Jingles" Rojanway Give Me A Call, MX, MXJ (Ch. Heronsway Freestyle UDT, HT, ROMX, VC, ex Sandwynn's Californiadreamer), is shown here with judge Anne Platt. (Photo by Kitten Rodwell)

of obstacles and the speed of the performance are increased. The difficulty of the course is also increased by setting up traps (two obstacles very close to one another), call-offs (an incorrect obstacle directly in the dog's path; the dog must be called off with a directional command to turn toward the correct obstacle), and difficult approaches.

The AKC also has Jumpers with Weaves, which is a course with no contact obstacles. Instead, it has jumps and weave poles, and may or may not have open and/or closed tunnels. Titles in JWW include Novice, Open, Excellent and Master Excellent.

All three organizations have similar rules and obstacles, but their emphasis may be in different areas. For instance, the AKC does not consider going "wrong course" (in which the dog takes an obstacle in the wrong order) as seriously as the

other two organizations. With the USDAA and the NADAC, if a dog goes wrong course, he will not qualify. With the AKC, a Novice or Open dog can go wrong course twice, and an Excellent A dog can go wrong course once, and still qualify. Only the Excellent B dog will not qualify.

When it comes to refusals, however, the AKC is tougher. Refusals is a term for when a dog hesitates or refuses before performing an obstacle, or if he "runs out" or "runs by" and must circle back to approach the obstacle again. The NADAC does not judge refusals at any level because the time wasted probably will prevent the dog from qualifying anyway. With the USDAA, refusals are not judged at the Novice level, are judged only for the contact obstacles at the Advanced level and the weave poles and are judged at all obstacles at the Master level. With the AKC, all refusals are judged at every level, but you still can qualify in the Novice level with two refusals and in the Open level with one refusal. No refusals are allowed at the Excellent level.

The AKC does not allow weave poles in Novice agility, but it does require them in Novice JWW. The USDAA and the NADAC have a short set of weave poles at the Novice level, but refusals are not faulted.

Anne Platt, an agility judge for both the AKC and the NADAC, competes with Corgis. She and "Jingles" (Rojanway Give Me A Call, AX, CGC) placed seventh at the Excellent level for the AKC

Weave poles are one of the hardest things to learn. Tafarnwr GreenWoods Bechan, MX, AXJ, known as "Becky," makes it look easy. Becky, owned by Ken Boyd, won the 12-inch division at the national championships of the AKC, the NADAC, and the USDAA in 1997. (Photo by Tien Tran)

in 1998, and placed fourth in the 1999 USDAA National Agility Trial. Jingles has two daughters who also have formal agility titles. Anne finds that the hardest part of training Corgis is the problem of knocking down bars at the jumps. Because Corgis can easily jump the 12 inches, she is not sure if it is because they just don't mind knocking the bar, or if they tend to flatten out when at top speed, causing the bar to be knocked over. She says teaching them that it's better to go over than through the jump is harder than she ever thought it would be.

The A-frame also can be difficult for Corgis with their short legs. Start with the A-frame set low, and be patient. Don't do a lot of repetitions at the beginning, and let the dog gain confidence. If the dog is very motivated by food, you can bait the far side of the A-frame.

It is also generally agreed that the weave poles are hard for any dog to learn. Get your own set of poles, and train your dog at home; class once a week is not enough for learning this obstacle. Ken Boyd, whose Corgi, Becky, won the USDAA grand prix, the NADAC Elite Champion Agility Competition and the AKC National Championship 12-inch divisions all in a single year, has this to say for agility training: "Keep the dog's weight down and your attitude up!" He also feels that most herding dogs do so well and learn so quickly in agility that it's "almost cheating" to use them.

Agility is a very challenging and complex sport, but as dogs gain confidence, they can perform with almost the same speed at which they chase a ball. This speed can be a problem at advanced levels because they may miss the yellow contact zone coming off an obstacle. (With contact obstacles, there is a "contact zone" both going onto and coming off of the obstacle. This is to prevent potentially harmful jumps on and off.) The best advice is to put the time in at the Novice level to make sure that you get a solid contact so that this does not become a problem at advanced levels. It's also a good idea to wait a bit and not push the dog too hard. A dog may not compete until it is 12 months old, and it is a good idea to wait until the dog is 18 months to 2 years old before actually competing. This gives both the handler and the dog time to get in proper condition and build up stamina.

If you decide that agility is the sport for you, get the most current set of rules, and check Web sites for changes and additions. In the case of the AKC, for instance, the current brochure has no information about the Master Agility Championship. Next, find a club where you can train. You'll want the advice and guidance of a qualified instructor as you learn the best and safest way to teach your Corgi to navigate the obstacles. Besides, many of the obstacles are fairly expensive, and an agility course covers a lot of ground. Few people have the space to set up a complete course.

HERDING TRAINING

Herding is another area for fun with your Corgi, and it, too, is becoming more popular. Herding tests the Corgi's natural instincts on corralling ducks, sheep or cattle. It doesn't require much equipment, but it does require livestock and space!

Herding requires livestock, space and maybe a good map. (Drawing by Pat Rapple/Funny Bones)

Herding tests are a good way to see if your dog has what it takes for future herding trials. Clubs often have herding seminars in which dogs are tested to see if they have herding instinct. Failing one of these does not necessarily mean that your dog can't herd. If the dog is not used to livestock or to running free, this may be a very strange event. Sometimes it takes three or four exposures to get a dog comfortable with livestock. It is also not true that Corgis were only "driving" dogs—Corgis were "drover" dogs, which helped get stock to market. A "drover" can drive, fetch, and do boundary work, all while being a market dog.

While your dog may exhibit a desire to chase or move livestock, this is not the same as herding. If you feel that this is a sport that you want to

"Rave" (Iverness Llanelly's Rave On) keeps a cow moving in the right direction . . . (Photo by Lucy E. Jones, DVM)

Sheep are no problem for Desperado's Young Gun, PT, CD, owned by Karen Sheppard. (Photo by Linda Leeman/ EWE-TOPIA)

. . . and with help from two buddies (Llanelly's Columbine, and Am./Can. Ch. Llanelly's Carillon), sends the rest of the herd toward the barn. (Photo by Lucy E. Jones, DVM)

Desperado's Young Gun, PT, CD, owned by Karen Sheppard, moves these sheep to a new location. Owner: Karen Sheppard. (Photo by Linda Leeman/Ewe-Topia)

pursue, find a training school that will help you and your dog develop into a herding team. As with any class or school, check out how the class is run and the staff's attitude toward various breeds. A trainer who thinks that only Border Collies or Australian Cattle Dogs can herd is not going to help you get the best from your Corgi.

Herding titles included Started, Intermediate and Advanced. As in obedience training, a dog must pass under three different judges and with a score of no less than half the available points in any single area judged. A herding championship can also be earned by any dog that has a Herding Excellent (HX) title and who earns 15 championship points in Advanced classes, with at least two first places under two different judges. Points earned are based on the number of dogs defeated.

Write or call the AKC for its pamphlet on herding for a complete list of rules and regulations.

TRACKING TRAINING

Tracking is another choice in the list of things to do with your Corgi. It doesn't take much in the way of equipment—just a harness and a 40-foot lead—but it does take some wide-open spaces for laying track, and a good supply of hot dogs!

Tracking tests a dog's ability at scent discrimination and tests his stamina and perseverance over various terrains. In Variable Surface Tracking (VST), the terrain includes pavement as well as two other surfaces. The level of tracking (Tracking Dog, Tracking Dog Excellent and Variable Surface Tracking) determines the number of turns, the length of the trail, and how long the trail has "aged" before the dog starts the trail.

Care must be taken when training so that the trail is not crossed or otherwise contaminated by scents other than that of the track-layer. To begin with, the handler crushes the grass and places a hot dog in each footprint to make a simple trail. This marks the trail in three ways: with the handler scent, crushed vegetation, and the hot dog. At the end of the trail is something the dog will be happy to find. A glove with more hot dog is common, but the prize also could be a favorite toy. Gradually, trails get longer, include turns and are aged.

For the Tracking Dog (TD) title, a track is at least 440 yards long, has three to five turns, and has been aged at least 30 minutes. For a Tracking Dog Excellent (TDX) title, the track is at least 800 yards long, has five to seven turns and has been aged at least three hours. The TDX track also has four articles to be found, and a cross track is laid that, as the name implies, crosses the primary track. Variable Surface Tracking (VST) tests the dog's ability to track over changing surfaces. The VST test specifies three different surfaces, with one being vegetation and the other

At the end of the trail is something the dog will be happy to find—in this case, the bun and mustard to go with the hot dogs! (Drawing by Pat Rapple/Funny Bones)

two being concrete, asphalt, gravel, sand, hard pan or mulch.

The track is aged at least three hours and must have between four and eight turns.

Corgi owners who do tracking find Corgis easy to train. The dogs have good noses, are eager to trail, have a good coat for rough underbrush and have the stamina and endurance of a big dog. The only drawback is their short legs, which can mean quite a scramble over a fallen tree. If the dog must go around the obstacle, it may risk losing the scent.

Ch. Elfwish Nicholas Nickelby, CD, Can TD, HC, has no trouble with this track. (Photo by David Ermer)

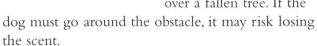

Nottingham's Monkey In the Middle, CD, NA, tries to find a track. (Photo by David Ermer)

Owner/trainer Lisa Ermer teaches Nottingham's Monkey in the Middle, CD, NA, to "down" when she successfully finds the article at the end of the track. (Photo by David Ermer)

A tracking title is won when two judges certify that the dog has successfully completed the track for any given trial. A Champion Tracker (C.T.) title is awarded to any dog that has all three tracking titles, TD, TDX and VST.

As with all the other performance events, get a copy of the regulations. While you could probably learn to track by yourself, finding someone who is experienced will speed the process and prevent mistakes in training.

VERSATILITY AWARDS

In 1990, the PWCCA developed the Versatile Corgi Award, with dogs earning points for this award in the areas of herding, tracking, obedience, agility and conformation. Corgis must participate in at least three areas—two of them being performance events—for a Versatile Corgi (VC) award. For a Versatile Corgi Excellent (VCX) award, they must have participated in four areas (at least three performance events) and earned the highest title in one of those performance events. A dog must earn 20 points for a VC award and 24 for a VCX. For example, a Conformation Championship is worth six points, a CD is worth four points, a CDX is worth six points and a UD is worth 10 points. Although these awards are presented by the PWCCA, any competing Corgi is eligible; the owner does not have to be a member of the PWCCA.

The first year for a Most Versatile Corgi award was 1999, and the award was open to any dog attending the National Specialty show. This award encourages entry in multiple events, with points awarded in each area. The dog accumulating the most points wins the Most Versatile Corgi award.

SERVICE DOG TRAINING

This is not an area the casual Corgi owner will be getting into, but it is an important area and one that all Corgi owners should be proud of. This type of training demonstrates the intelligence and willingness to work that characterizes this wonderful breed.

Joan Guertin, of Common Sense Dog Training in Branson, Missouri, trains Corgis as service dogs for the hearing—impaired. She says that anything you can teach them, they can do. In training, she uses a ball or a squeaky toy, or something else with

Service dogs do a lot of long downs, as Hi-Desert Piper ("Piper") illustrates. (Photo by Jeff B. Long)

a very specific sound. When the dog hears the sound, it knows it will receive a reward. Gradually, the dog connects that special sound with the sound he is being taught to become alert to.

A service dog should work silently and is trained to go to the hearing-impaired person and then lead that person to the sound. Most dogs will respond to a sound, but the job of the trainer is to teach them to take a person to the sound. The one exception is the sound of a fire alarm or a smoke detector. Then the dog alerts the owner and drops into a down.

Corgis teach themselves many behaviors specific to their own situation. A Corgi named Piper taught himself to alert his owner if anything was boiling dry. The sound of a teakettle is a sound hearing service dogs are taught to become alert to, but Piper didn't like the sound of a kettle's whistle,

Piper receives a reward for taking his trainer to the telephone when it rings.

so he would sound the alert just as the water boiled, and before there was enough steam to make the kettle shriek. This transferred to anything that was boiling, and has eliminated pans boiling dry in his household.

Guertin found that teaching Piper the basics was easy because he modeled the actions of another of her dogs, Flash (Ch. Hi-Desert Jump 'N Jak Flash, CGC). Guertin has since found that training time is cut when she trains any dog with

Flash because the dog in training learns by watching Flash.

A very important job for a service dog is alerting someone to the sound of an alarm clock or a clock radio. Guertin has found that her Corgis have a sense of time and don't even need the clock. For instance, if Flash wakes her up and she tells him that she's going to sleep for five more minutes, that's exactly how long he waits. She can tell him anything from five minutes to an hour.

For example, when she was away on a trip, she needed to get up at 5:30 A.M. rather than her normal time of 6 A.M. She placed a wakeup call at the motel's front desk, and then she told Flash that she needed to get up at 5:30. Flash woke her three minutes before the official wakeup call came.

Guertin also has found that dogs develop their own style of working. Piper is a highly motivated, very active dog, yet he wakes people with gentle little kisses. In contrast, Flash, who is very laid-back in his work, leaps on the bed and slobbers all over them. He pushes with his head and feet, and if Guertin rolls over, he uses his nose to root under her neck until he can get his body underneath; then he sits her up. (Ironically, she found this very useful last winter, when she fell and cracked a rib, and found getting into a sitting position difficult.)

Besides alerting someone to sounds, a service dog may be asked for something more. Piper's owner dropped her keys and, because she did not hear them drop, went on without them. She wondered whether Guertin could teach Piper to tell her when she dropped something. So, Guertin developed a game around dropping things, and Piper now happily picks up anything his mistress drops.

Service dogs offer more than just a way to know about sounds or retrieve lost items.

At a presentation for children, Flash demonstrates his technique for waking up owner Joan Guertin. (Photo by Kathryn Buck/Springfield, Missouri, New-Leader)

Piper has learned to retrieve dropped items. (Photo by MGW Newspaper, Sacramento, California)

Piper retrieves his mistress's hat when the wind blows it off. (Photo by Joan Guertin)

For any service dog, including Piper and his friend, grocery store visits are a part of the training. (Photo by Joan Guertin)

One owner was always afraid to take walks by herself because she couldn't hear and was never sure if someone might be approaching from behind. Now, with her Corgi service dog, she enjoys evening walks around the neighborhood.

Sondra Douglas received Hi-Desert Evening Star of CCI, known as "Evie," from Canine Companions for Independent Living. She had never had a service dog before, but her increasing loss of hearing was also leading to a loss of confidence. Douglas was staying inside more and was apprehensive about travel. At first, when the idea of a Corgi came up, her response was, "They're ugly, and I want a bigger dog." Now, however, she

adores Evie and her talents, and she can't imagine having any other breed.

With Evie, Douglas has traveled on planes and trains and even has visited Disneyland. Evie goes everywhere with her and wears a smart little jacket proclaiming her a service dog, but Douglas still sometimes encounters problems with businesses that don't want to let her enter with a dog. She attributes this to the fact that she does not have a

Sondra Douglas with Evie (Hi-Desert Evening Star of CCI). (Photo by Joan Guertin)

visible handicap, but she does suggest gently that people could take the time to read the dog's jacket.

Outside, Douglas relies on Evie's body language to tell her what is going on outside the range of Douglas's vision. She watches Evie's ears, and that tells her if someone is approaching from the rear. Also, when grocery shopping, Evie will pull Douglas back from a blind corner if another cart is coming their way.

When Douglas's parents were ill, she also taught Evie to come and get her if her parents rang a small dinner bell. She finds that the more she asks of Evie, the more Evie does.

Canine Companions for Independent Living recertifies its service dogs every three years, evaluating how the person handles the dog and making sure that the dogs are still steady and dependable.

THERAPY DOG TRAINING

Therapy is another important area in which dogs help people just by being dogs. A visit to a nursing home with your Corgi can brighten the lives of the residents, and there's not much needed on your part. It helps if your dog has had some obedience lessons or has its CGC title—some organizations actually certify therapy dogs—but almost any well-mannered dog can visit a nursing home. The biggest disadvantage with a Corgi is that sometimes it is hard for the residents to reach the dog to pet it, and jumping up is frowned on if the person is older and frail. I usually just scoop up the dog and hold it close to the person.

Many all-breed clubs include visiting nursing homes as part of their outreach programs, and the AKC also encourages school visits to educate children in dog care and handling.

John Monroe-Cassel made some interesting discoveries about dogs and people while he was the co-pastor of the First Baptist Church in Bainbridge, New York. He found that frequently people had trouble grieving; they sincerely missed the deceased but could not seem to let any of their emotions out. Talking about the loved one's pet with them was the quickest way to get the people in touch with their feelings.

When people talk about their pets, the genuine emotions are uncluttered by associations in

The Corgi certainly is versatile! When "Flash" (Ch. Hi-Desert Jump 'N Jak Flash, CGC) is not helping owner Joan Guertin with service dog work, he's busy winning at dog shows. Pictured here winning Best in Show, in 1999, he ranked number 8 in show rankings.

Emotions regarding pets are not cluttered with guilt, because a dog never judges. (Photo by Winter/Churchill)

people's relationships. The feeling of loss is not there until the pet association is made. Talking about a specific pet brought people to a level of honesty. Frequently, there is a lot of guilt over a death, which makes it harder to talk about. Starting with the pet as a reference circumvents those guilt feelings. Emotions regarding pets are not cluttered with guilt, because a dog never judges.

In another situation dealing with troubled adults, Monroe-Cassel said that the only time one of the group members was ever really lucid was when talking about her dog, and she would talk about herself in relation to her dog.

Dogs become family members and are a very real part of a family. People are frequently more apt to grieve openly and totally over a dog that dies than a person because there is no guilt; there are no relationship entanglements.

Whether you have a cuddly couch potato whose only job is keeping your feet warm and your blood pressure down, or an agility whiz who helps keep you as fit and trim as she is, a Corgi is a wonderful addition to the family.

Am./Can. Ch. Horoko Caralon Dickens, ROMX (Am./Can. Ch. Schaferhaus Yul B of Quanda, ROMX, ex Am./Can. Ch. Caralon's Q-T Hot Wheels, ROM), known as "Dickens," currently is the top stud dog of Pembroke Welsh Corgis and has sired more than 70 Champions. (Photo by Downey Dog Show Photography)

CHAPTER 11

Headliners

Corgis command the spotlight both inside and outside the show ring. In the show ring, or taking part in performance events, the Corgi is the equal of any other breed of dog, but they also can show up center stage in other areas.

CELEBRITY CORGIS

One of the best-known owners of Corgis is Elizabeth II, Queen of England. Since 1933, Britain's royal family has had Corgis. The Queen's first Corgi, known as "Dookie," was formally known as Rozavel Golden Eagle, later to be joined by Rozavel Lady Jane. Corgis still live at Buckingham Palace today as well as at the Queen Mother's residence, Clarence House.

Olympic diver Greg Louganis, who won gold medals in springboard and platform diving at both the 1984 and 1988 Olympics, also co-owns and shows Corgis with Kathleen and Rick Mallery of Castell Corgis. Horror writer Stephen King has a Corgi as well—let's hope it wasn't the inspiration for *Cujo!*

Corgis also frequently provide the subject matter for author-artist Tasha Tudor, who is known for her delicate watercolors, quaint period settings, and Corgis. In her illustrated version of *A Night Before Christmas,* a delightful Corgi romps with St. Nicholas, inspects the toys and even helps fill the stockings. *Corgiville Fair* and *The Great Corgiville Kidnapping* feature an entire community of Corgis and include some famous Corgi kennel names in "Hilden's" Hardware and "Cote de Neige" beauty aids.

117

Olympic gold medallist Greg Louganis co-owns Am./Can. Ch. Castell Can't Touch This "Trev'r" with Kathleen and Rick Mallery. (Photo by Castell Corgis)

A Corgi also is the main character in a novel by Emily Carmichael, *Finding Mr. Right*. In this romance novel, a woman who has been murdered comes back as a Corgi to help her best friend find the perfect husband. Author Rita Mae Brown, with the help of her cat, Sneaky Pie Brown, also has written a series of mystery stories that feature a cat and a Corgi: In 1998, Disney Studios produced a made-for-TV movie called *Murder, She Purred*, based on the Brown book, *Rest in Pieces*. The movie actually used three Corgis: Baci, the main Corgi, and two "doubles," Thomas and Murphy.

CORGIS AS ACTORS

Cheryl Harris, who works for Birds and Animals Unlimited, owned by Gary Gero, was one of the animal trainers for the movie *Murder, She Purred*. Harris is a trainer with more than 20 years of experience, but this was the first time that she had ever worked with Corgis. She found them "wonderful" and has high praise for their intelligence, stability and temperament. "They really are a big dog," she said.

Unlike the Corgis in the 1950s Disney movie *Little Dog Lost*, none of the Corgis used in this move were related. The main Corgi, Baci, whose name means "kiss" in Italian, and who was named after an Italian candy similar to a Hershey's Kiss, is owned by Sue Humphrey (who also works for Birds and Animals Unlimited). Baci's double, Thomas, who had a soulful look, was leased to the trainers by Gwen Platt because he looked exactly like Baci. Murphy, a fluffy owned by Debbie Pearl, was the "designated jumper." He had great attitude and was very athletic, but it took quite a bit of hair styling (and cutting) and makeup to make him look like Baci.

Humphrey finds Corgis very sharp, yet totally manageable. Her only criticism is that if one Corgi is being petted, another often shoves the first away to get his share! They also can be aggressive with other dogs when it comes to food, although

Humphrey has never had a problem with the dogs being aggressive toward people.

To train her dogs, Humphrey starts them young with retrieving and uses positive reinforcement with lots of praise; she saves food for getting "cute looks" out of her furry actors.

Harris starts with basic obedience with the dogs she trains. Because the hardest thing to teach a dog is go away from people, she incorporates that into almost everything else. She sends the dog a little way away and then instructs him to do a down stay. She then uses lots of food and praise, and although she uses a clicker with other animals, she uses this tool only when teaching something very tricky with a dog. This is not because a clicker doesn't work well with dogs, but Harris finds that most dogs respond so well to food and praise that it's just easier not to have to worry about the tool.

Baci appears here as his character, "Tucker," with co-star "Mrs. Murphy" in the Disney made-for-TV movie Murder, She Purred. *(Photo by Disney Studios)*

Birds and Animals Unlimited has a large ranch where the company's animals stay, but Harris also has a place with 5 acres and a 1-acre fenced yard. In fact, during the training for *Murder, She Purred*, all the Corgis stayed with her. The filming was done in Toronto, and Harris rented a house near a wonderful walking path.

Actually, Thomas spent the nights with another handler, Tammy Blackburn, who says that he was not content just to sleep in the bed with her—he had to have his head on the pillow! This was Blackburn's first time working with Corgis, and she says she was "blown away" at how quickly the dogs learned, and how good-natured and loving they were.

Harris and the other trainers try to find out what each individual dog does best or enjoys doing most. That way, they can be sure to cast the dogs doing the things at which they excel. Baci is a good actor; he doesn't mind holding still and hits his mark every time. Thomas likes to keep moving, which is why he was used for all the action shots.

The dogs had five weeks to prepare and four weeks to shoot the film. During this time, the cat and Baci became such good friends that the cat wanted to rub up against the dog even at times when this wasn't called for.

Thomas (Brookshire Royal Flush, OA) was one of the Corgi "doubles" in Murder, She Purred. *Thomas is a Hersonsway Free Style grandson. (Photo by Gwen Platt)*

Corgis make the headlines internationally, too: Am./Jap. Ch. Lorjen It's A Guy Thing (Ch. Lamin Rumor Has It ex Ch. Blaidd Amanda Cross) was the no. 1 Pembroke Welsh Corgi in Japan in 1998 and won Best in Show at the Asian International Dog Show in 1999. (Photo courtesy of Lorjen)

Some dogs come to the trainers with some training, but Harris says that most house pets are trained *not* to do the very things that dogs frequently are trained to do, including jumping on the couch, tipping over wastebaskets and rummaging in the garbage. As the dog becomes better trained, he learns to think and then learns even more.

In *Murder, She Purred,* the animals actually "talked" to each other, which added another element of difficulty to the training: The animals had to look at each other and look like they were relating to each other. In this instance, the humans trained the cat to look at a trainer and to ignore activity behind it. The dog was trained to look at the cat and also to ignore activity behind it.

The most important elements in training, according to Harris, are patience and consistency, as well as having fun. It's also important to learn the tools you need to help the dog understand what you want him to do. Sometimes you also can build on mistakes—the main thing is not to get angry at mistakes. After all, people learn through mistakes, and so do dogs. Harris never corrects a dog until she knows that the animal knows what is expected. She also rarely uses the word "no," instead leaving it for really hard corrections, such as aggression. Otherwise, she says a softer "uh, uh," or "ah, ah." Or, she'll say, "Would you like to try that again?"

Interestingly, Harris finds it is easier to teach a dog to stay when the dog is up on something, for two reasons. One is that if the dog breaks a stay while it is up on something, it is very obvious; the other is that it seems to be easier for the dog to understand the concept when he is off the ground.

Becky (Tafarnwr Greenwoods Bechen, MX, AXJ), owned by Ken Boyd, shows her winning form in agility on the dog walk and over different jumps. (Photos by Tien Tran)

CORGIS AS SHOW DOGS

A Corgi's intelligence and working ability help make it a winner in fiction—and in fact. In 1997, Ken Boyd and his Corgi, Becky (Tafarnwr Greenwoods Bechen, MX, AXJ), won the Agility National Championships in the 12-inch division in the AKC nationals, the USDAA Grand Prix National Championship and the NADAC nationals.

In the conformation ring, Corgis are also winners. Judges are becoming educated to the merits of these little dogs and dedicated breeders are producing sturdy, well-built animals that are earning placements in the group ring and, more and more frequently, going Best in Show. Top-quality Corgis are earning Register of Merit and Register of Merit Excellent awards from the Pembroke Welsh Corgi Club of America.

OTCH Welshberri's Belle of the Ball was the first Pembroke Welsh Corgi to become an Obedience Trial Champion, in 1981. (Photo courtesy of Tania Nagro)

Ch. and OTCH Aberdare Eliza of Taliesin, UD. (Photo courtesy of Peggy McConnell)

These awards go to dogs that have passed on their quality, as indicated by the number of Champion offspring they have. Males must have produced 10 Champions to gain the ROM after their name and 15 for ROMX. Bitches must produce five and eight Champions, respectively.

In obedience competition, OTCH Welshberi Belle of the Ball, UD, owned by Titiana Nagro, was the first Corgi to achieve the Obedience championship (OTCH title). The first male was OTCH Garvins Grandmaster Freddie, UDT (Utility Dog Tracking), trained by Evelyn Bock, DVM. The first

bitch to be awarded an OTCH who was also a conformation champion was Ch. and OTCH Aberdare Eliza of Taliesin, UD (Utility Dog), with owner-trainer Peggy McConnell. The first male was Ch. and OTCH Backacres Bud In Ski, UD, who was owned and trained by Barbara "Bobbe" Morris.

While there have been subtle changes in the breed over the years, a look at the pictures of some of the dogs of the 1950s and earlier shows that quality stands the test of time. Look at the head of Eng. Ch. Crymmych President, and all of Lees Symphony. Ch. Willets Red Jacket could win today, as could other "old-timers."

An informal poll of Corgi breeders who were asked what dogs and/or bloodlines contributed

The first Versatility Corgi was Ch. Blujor Sio Calako Kachina, CDX, TDX, HT, Can. CD, VCX. (Photo by Hanks)

"Buddy" Ch. and OTCH Backacher's Bud-In-Ski, UD (Ch. Lost Hills Rocky Road ex Sheffields Bright Lil Cory), is shown here with owner/trainer Bobbe Morris.

greatly to the breed garnered much praise for Ch. Willets Red Jacket and for the Cote de Neige Corgis, with special mention of Ch. Cote de Neige Pennysaver ROMX; Ch. Cote de Neige Chance of Fox Run, ROMX; and Ch. Cote de Neige Instant Replay, ROMX. One breeder pointed out that Pennysaver was closer to the current type, being a bit longer and heavier than many Corgis before.

More recent favorites are Ch. Bear Acres Mister Snowshoes, UD, ROM; Ch. Schaferhaus Yul B of Quanda, ROMX; Ch. Wey Smut; Ch. Belroyd Seabird, ROMX; Eng. Ch. Belroyd Nut Cracker,

who passed on his lovely head; and Am. & Can. Ch. Blaizwood Hooray Henry, CDX, ROM, who was admired for his handsome head, wonderfully large and strong ears, dark eye rims, great neck and shoulders and wonderful side movement. Ch. Heronsway Freestyle, UDT, HT, ROMX, VC, is another contemporary dog who has not only excelled in obedience, tracking and herding, but has also excelled as a stud dog, passing on his traits as an excellent example of the breed and also passing on his intelligence and ability to compete in performance events. Am. & Can. Ch. Horoko Caralon Dickens, ROMX (Am. Can. Ch. Schaferhaus Yul B of Quanda, ROMX, ex Am. Can. Ch. Caralon's Q-T Hot Wheels ROM), is currently the top stud dog in Pembroke Welsh Corgis, having sired more than 70 Champions.

Ch. Willets Red Jacket. (Photo by Tauskey)

Ch. Belroyd Seabird, ROMX (Tweedbanks Portland Bill ex Belroyd Popinjay), was the sire of nearly 30 Champions. (Photo by Sandyshire Corgis)

Eng. Ch. Belroyd Nut Cracker (Pemland Royal Command ex Eng. Ch. Belroyd Jacana) was an influential sire both in England and in the United States. (Photo by Fall)

I have a soft spot for dogs from the Nebriowa kennel of Tim Mathiesen and the late Larry Cunha. My first love from their line was Ch. Nebriowa Coco Chanel. The topline and movement of the Nebriowa line is absolutely wonderful, and these dogs are leaving their mark on dogs in the ring today.

The efforts of the early breeders with kennel names such as Rozavel, Stormerbank, Cote de Neige, Revelmere, Wey, Hildenmanor, Lees, Kaytop, Blands and Bowhit can be seen in the dogs of today. With prefixes of Festiniog, Nebriowa,

Shaferhaus, Heronsway, the list goes on, and for every kennel mentioned, someone will say, "But what about . . .?" or "How could you leave out . . .?" And they would be right. Today's Corgi breeders are, if anything, more conscientious about their breeding programs than ever before. Breeding "the best to the best" today means not just physical beauty and impressive show wins, but utilizing OFA, CERF and DNA testing that the dogs produced are as healthy as possible.

Ch. Heronsway Free Style UDT, HT, ROMX, VC (Ch. Happiharbor Tom of Hersonsway ex Ch. Heronsway Free Spirit), known as "Tyler." Owner: Tibby Chase. (Photo by Terry Reynolds)

who can easily make the transition from couch to conformation, and pet to performance—they always are willing to try anything, and they still are eager to be a person's best friend.

This book has tried to introduce the reader to all the best in Corgis, from all areas of Corgi endeavors, but it is the dedicated breeders who really give the best and who make sure that those who acquire their puppies are getting a healthy, good-tempered, sturdy,

Temperament is another important part of the breeding program, and it has not been neglected. Corgis are still bright, fearless, friendly little dogs intelligent dog that can excel in any task set before him. These breeders, past and present, are the true "headliners."

To produce generations of quality is one of the reasons breeders breed. Left to right, these dogs are five generations of bitches: Ch. Lamin Bachelor Affair, Ch. Valleyvixen Autumn Whisper, Ch. Valleyvixen Sunrunner, Am./Can. Ch. Valleyvixen Sunrunners Colors and Can. Ch. Sunrunners Kodak Royal. (Photo by A-N PRODUCTIONS/Tom and Linda Nutting)

CHAPTER 12

Breeding

Breeding is a decision that should not be made lightly. Many good dogs are available, and many more are being bred every day. Just wanting to replace the beloved family pet is not a good-enough reason to breed. My second Corgi, Heather, was a wonderful dog. She was loving and gentle, and good with other dogs and all people. As a Corgi, however, she was a disaster; she was too high in the rear, had a domed head, did not have great feet and had a bad front. I had her spayed at 6 months of age. She was a terrific dog—I'd love to have another like her—but she was not a good Corgi, and breeding her would not have been a good thing for the breed.

Let's take a look at some solid arguments for—and against—breeding. Be sure to think long and hard before breeding. This isn't a decision that you can just jump into.

REASONS FOR BREEDING

Just having a dog that is "show-quality" is not a reason to breed. While the temptation to have puppies "just like Honey" is great, you must resist. For one thing, there is no guarantee that Honey's puppies will be anything like her at all. For another, there are lots of wonderful dogs out there. No dog will ever "replace" a dog you love—all are different and wonderful in their own way.

If you think you'd like to breed to "make back the money," think again. While a litter may occasionally make money for the breeder, this is not generally true. If you figure in the cost of the bitch; the cost

Corgi puppies asleep are almost as cute as Corgi puppies awake. (Photo by Kathryn Smith)

of the stud fee; shipping fees to get the bitch to the stud; fees for artificial insemination or for frozen semen (if that turns out to be the best way to go); costs for brucellosis testing, hip X-rays to check for dysplasia, eye tests and von Willebrand's testing; extra visits to the veterinarian to make sure that the bitch is pregnant and healthy; the possible cost of a C-section; costs for docking tails and removing dew claws; worming medicines; vaccinations; and loss of your vacation time to be able to properly care for bitch and puppies, you will be lucky to break even. And this doesn't count the emotional investment. There is a chance that you will lose one or more puppies. There is a chance that you might lose the mother. Is this a price you are willing to pay?

If you want to breed a litter so that the children can witness the "miracle of birth," are you also prepared for them to see the "miracle of death"? There's nothing cuter than a litter of healthy Corgi pups, and there's nothing sadder than losing them one by one in spite of all your efforts. One long-time breeder, in a moment of frustration over a lost litter, said, "If I could find the person who told me that having puppies was fun, I'd nail him to a tree!" There are much easier, better ways for children to learn about birth—check out your local library for appropriate books and videos. Before you breed, talk to several breeders and listen to the pros and cons. Don't use your dog as a teaching aid.

If you are still determined to breed, do it for the right reasons: to improve the breed and your line, to pass on the positive points about your dog and to try to eliminate faults. Then start with advice and help from your breeder and your veterinarian. The breeder will know her line better than anyone will. If you have a bitch she can best advise you on the choice of stud dog to use. After all, going to the top dog in the country will not give you the best puppies if his faults are the same as hers. (Yes, he has faults; no dog is perfect.) And even with all the advice in the world, breeding is still a game of chance. The old saying, "Breed the best to the best and hope for the best," is still all the assurance you'll ever have.

If you have a male and would like to see him used at stud, he should probably be a finished champion. It is not absolutely necessary, but if a bitch owner is going to go to all the time, trouble and expense of breeding and whelping a litter and then raising that litter and placing the puppies, that owner probably will be looking for the added guarantee that the male is a good-enough representative of the breed to earn a championship.

THE BREEDING PROCESS

Before you breed your bitch, make sure that she has a checkup and is healthy. Do not breed before her second heat—in fact, most breeders suggest waiting until at least the third heat. Going by age, wait until the bitch is 18 months to 2 years of age before breeding. Most breeders prefer waiting until full maturity at 2 years. Your male should have a checkup, too, and it should include a sperm count.

Whether you own the male or the female, make sure both dogs are tested for brucellosis. Brucellosis is a disease that is hard to detect in adult dogs, which is why you must require a blood test before breeding. Brucellosis in the bitch can cause abortion or fetal resorption. Although a bitch may recover it is recommended not to breed a bitch that has ever tested positive because relapses are common with this disease. In males, infected dogs rarely recover and frequently become sterile. Treatment is with tetracyclines and gentamicin.

As with buying a puppy, there should be a written contract between the owners of both the bitch and the stud, to spell out what is expected on both sides. What is the fee? If it is reduced or waived in return for a puppy, what sex does the

Elfwish Little Jazz looks like she will take after her mother, Ch. Elfwish Jasmine, CD. (Photo by Sandra Wolfskill)

dog owner get, and who gets first pick? What if there is only one of whatever sex either party requests? Most contracts specify a refund of part (or all) of the stud fee if there is not a live litter. Be sure to spell out what constitutes a live litter: Is it one puppy? Two? Will you be paying board for the time your bitch is with the stud dog? (Traditionally, the bitch travels to the dog.) If artificial insemination is required, who pays the veterinarian's bill? Who pays for any extra charges for chilled or frozen semen? As with buying a puppy, there are many different arrangements that can be made. Just make sure everything is clearly understood before the breeding.

If you are the stud dog owner and the bitch is staying with you, make sure you have a safe, quiet place for her where she will not be bothered by other resident dogs.

Ideally, if the bitch is inexperienced, the stud dog should have been used before; if the stud is inexperienced, try to use him on an experienced bitch. Trying to breed two virgins makes it likely to be an awkward, frustrating experience for both of them (and you). Likewise, if this is *your* first time, line up some experienced help. The help doesn't have to be a Corgi breeder—just someone who has bred smaller dogs. Many Corgi breeders like to breed the dogs on a table for more control and because it's easier on their backs (the human's back, that is, not the dogs'). Whether you choose the table or the floor, make sure that the surface is nonslip so that the dogs are safe.

English Champion Belroyd Nut Cracker, seen here with the Working Group trophy at Crufts.

"Why are humans involved at all?" you may ask. Why not just put the dogs together and let nature take its course? For starters, if the dogs are strangers to each other, there may be initial aggression, rather than love at first sight, especially from the bitch. You don't want to risk either dog being bitten by the other. Also, you are either paying or receiving money for this service. You want results, which you are more apt to get if you don't leave the breeding to chance. If either dog is inexperienced, the presence of a person can be calming, and the person can also help things along, either by holding the bitch in position or helping to guide the male. Holding the dogs while they are tied can also help prevent injury, especially to the male.

Bitches vary as to when they are receptive, but generally, they are ready to be bred between the tenth and sixteenth days of their season. They will usually not accept a male if they are not ready. Most breeders try for two breedings. Vaginal smears done by your veterinarian can help pinpoint the right time, which is especially important if you are using artificial insemination. If you are using chilled or frozen semen, you will want to make sure both that your bitch is absolutely ready and that your veterinarian is qualified to perform this service. With frozen semen, insemination is frequently done surgically, depositing the semen directly into the uterus. With chilled or a fresh collection, the semen is usually inserted through the vagina with a syringe.

Although using these last two procedures is expensive, it may be cheaper than shipping, is less stressful for the bitch and may provide access to a stud dog that would otherwise be unavailable (such as one that lives in a foreign country or is deceased).

After all the effort, is your bitch pregnant? It can be hard to tell, especially early on. Some bitches will experience mild morning sickness. Some will go off their feed for a while. At around the twenty-ninth day, your vet may be able to tell you if the bitch is pregnant by abdominal palpation. Watch for weight gain; see if the animal "looks pregnant." Mammary glands begin to swell around the thirty-fifth day. Some bitches go through a false pregnancy, however, complete with a rounded tummy, enlarged mammaries, and nesting habits, which can really confuse things.

The usual gestation period for dogs is between fifty-eight and sixty-six days, and sixty-three days seems to be the norm for Corgis. Start taking the bitch's temperature three or four days before her due date. When the temperature starts to drop, she is getting ready to whelp.

In the best of all possible worlds, your breeder will be there for you. If the distance makes daily phone calls prohibitive, try to find someone locally who can act as a mentor. My breeder was about 400 miles away, but fortunately a kennel club member was a long-time breeder of Lhasa Apsos. Some breed-specific information still required long-distance calls, but much basic advice and support came from the Lhasa breeder. Also invest in a good book, such as *The Joy of Breeding Your Own Show Dog*, by Anne Seranne, and *Successful Dog Breeding: The Complete Handbook of Canine*

Like father, like son: Am./Can. Ch. Blaizewood Hooray Henry, CDX (Jason), appears to be taking after his sire, Eng. Ch. Belroyd Nut Cracker, with his winning ways. (Photo by Bernard Kernan)

Midwifery, by Chris Walkowicz and Bonnie Wilcox, DVM. These two books particularly are invaluable.

THE WHELPING PROCESS

This is not the time to start wondering where she will give birth and what you might need. Set up a whelping box well in advance in a quiet, warm area away from the other dogs. Make sure that there's room for you nearby because you will want to sleep near the box for at least the first week. The first seven days are usually the most crucial. With my litter, the last puppy born was so small that she had trouble hanging onto a nipple. One nudge from another puppy, and she'd lose her grip.

I spent the first week holding her onto the nipple so that she could feed. It's always something!

The Whelping Box

You can make a whelping box, buy one, or use a child's wading pool or the bottom of a large crate. For Corgis, a box that is 30 to 36 inches square is about right. Sides of 12 to 14 inches high will protect against drafts and keep heat in.

Many commercial whelping boxes have a "pig rail," a board that runs around the bottom of the box that provides a space for a puppy but that keeps the mother from accidentally crushing it between her body and the side of the box. This is a good addition if you are making a box, but Corgis are not as prone to this as some larger breeds.

Some ready-made boxes are plastic, which makes for easy cleaning and disinfecting, and some also have a hollow in the middle where the pups can cluster and which can easily be heated. These are easier than dealing with heating pads or heat lamps, and the bitch can get away from the extra heat when she needs to. I didn't need to use either a heating pad or a lamp because our dining room was right over the wood-burning furnace area of the basement, so the heat rose directly into the dining room. With the doors closed, it was easy to maintain 85° at floor level.

A child's wading pool can make an easy-to-clean whelping box. (Photo by Susan Ewing)

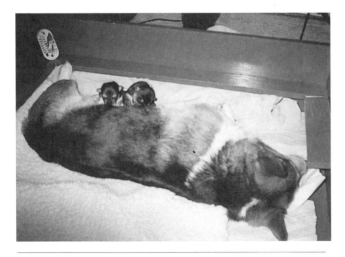

This mother and her puppies are in a whelping box with a "pig rail." Note the thermometer in the corner—the correct temperature is very important. (Photo by Kathryn Smith)

Llanelly's Little Sister Iris is content to have her puppies in a cardboard box. (Photo by Lucy E. Jones, DVM)

Inverness Llanelly's Rave On finds that a cardboard box makes a handy snack in addition to a good whelping box! (Photo by Lucy E. Jones, DVM)

When my bitch was pregnant, I ordered a wonderful plastic whelping box, but there was a mix-up on the order. Three days before her due date, I was without a box. Instead, I used a child's wading pool with pieces of lumber under it to make it slope toward the center and form a "nest." Layers of newspaper and pieces of fake fleece made the bed. This makeshift whelping box was easy to clean and easy to move, if necessary, and the sides were high enough to contain puppies but low enough for the bitch to easily jump in and out.

A separate heated box is a good idea to use when the puppies are being born. Also be sure to have extra towels, antiseptic, scissors, thread, nasal aspirator, surgical gloves and the two books I mentioned earlier.

Let the bitch get used to the box a few days ahead of time. When her temperature lowers and she shows physical signs of going into whelp by panting and rearranging all her smooth, clean bedding (an action called nesting), it's time to move her into the box. When my Megan started into whelp, she was perfectly happy to stay in the box while I sat nearby and reread *Successful Dog Breeding*.

The Birthing

Corgis average between two and six puppies, although more is not unheard of. One X-ray a week before the due date can give you an idea of how many to expect.

If all goes well, regularly spaced puppies will arrive and be happy and healthy. As they arrive, if the mother doesn't immediately do it, remove the sac surrounding the puppy, and rub the animal vigorously. Either allow the bitch to eat the placenta, or remove it. The general opinion seems to be to let the bitch eat two or three for nutritional value and to stimulate milk production. More than two or three may cause diarrhea. Of course, if your bitch has a C-section, she won't get any placenta, and that seems to be fine, too.

If a puppy is a bit large or there is a breech presentation (hind legs first), you may need help with the delivery. Use a rough towel to insure a good grip, and pull downward with the contractions.

If the mother's attentions are not enough to get the puppy breathing, you may need to help clear fluids from the lungs. Centrifugal force will help if you hold the puppy in both hands, supporting body and neck, and gently swing downward in an arc between your legs.

If you have someone helping you, and they are not a dog person, you should probably explain what you are doing. When my veterinarian instituted this maneuver, my friend gave me a look of pure horror, positive that the doctor had lost his mind.

If your bitch is in labor but no pups are being born, contact your veterinarian. It may be uterine inertia and require a shot of oxytocin; it could be a puppy, or puppies, stuck in the birth canal. Whatever it is, don't wait. Corgis are fairly stoic when it comes to pain, and a common mistake during whelping is to wait too long before calling for help. If it looks like there's a problem, or if you think the dog will require a C-section, don't mess around. Get to your veterinary clinic as soon as

possible. Minutes could make the difference in life or death for the mother or the puppies.

My Megan ended up whelping at the veterinarian's office, with the help of several shots of oxytocin. Oxytocin causes contractions and also causes milk to let down. For the final puppy, we needed a C-section. I took all the puppies home in a heated box and settled everyone into the whelping box, and Megan got on with being a mother. The first three puppies had nursed briefly before the C-section, but none had had very much to eat. The important thing was keeping them warm—a chilled puppy is a dead puppy. Of course, food is important, but it is secondary to warmth when puppies are newly born.

A C-section is stressful on both puppies and mother. Although it is not to be considered lightly, it should be done if it means saving the lives of the puppies or the dam. One C-section doesn't necessarily mean the bitch will always need one, but after two in a row, you might want to consider retiring her as a brood bitch.

Once the puppies are born, there can be other problems. The bitch may develop eclampsia. Eclampsia is not common, seen most frequently in toy breeds, but it can happen in any breed, and it is very serious. Eclampsia is a calcium deficiency and may be caused by calcium supplements. Although it seems logical that giving calcium supplements to a pregnant bitch would help in the milk-making process, in fact, it does just the reverse. Under ordinary circumstances, a hormone released by the parathyroid gland makes it possible for the body to easily access calcium stored in the bones. Too much calcium in the system can result in parathyroid gland atrophy. This, in turn, inhibits release of the hormone needed to utilize calcium in the body. The result is a calcium deficiency.

Symptoms may include irritability, restlessness, increased salivation, seizures and running a temperature. If strange behavior is noted, remove the pups for their safety. Treatment includes intravenous and/or subcutaneous administration of a calcium solution. This must be monitored by a veterinarian, because too rapid delivery of the calcium may cause heart failure. The bitch may also need to be cooled with ice or alcohol baths.

If the condition has been caught early, pups may again nurse, but they should be weaned from the mother by three weeks.

If eclampsia occurs in repeated litters, the bitch should be spayed, both for her sake, and because the tendency for eclampsia may be passed on to succeeding generations.

Mastitis may result if the puppies do not nurse at all the breasts. Mastitis is an infection of one or more mammary glands. Early signs include discomfort for the bitch when the puppies nurse, inflammation and masses between the glands. The bitch will be reluctant to nurse and will have a fever. Milk will be red or brown. Treatment includes a broad-spectrum antibiotic that is harmless to the puppies. Warm compresses applied to the infected gland and gentle stripping of the milk will ease discomfort and may help avert abscess and rupture of the gland.

Although puppies tend not to nurse at affected glands, great care should be taken. One breeder

Tired from play, with tummies full of puppy food, these puppies crash for a quick "pup-nap." (Photo by Lucy E. Jones, DVM)

with more than thirty years' experience only once had to deal with mastitis, and in that instance, the bitch was in such pain that she killed her entire litter. This breeder further reports that she milked pus from the infected glands for an entire week. Another breeder had the infected gland rupture.

Taking your bitch's temperature daily will alert you to any rise in temperature that may mean an infection.

It is possible for the bitch to just totally ignore the puppies and/or not produce any milk at all. That means it is up to you to feed the puppies. You can bottle-feed or tube feed. With tube feeding, a small rubber tube is inserted into the puppy's stomach and the formula is "injected" with a syringe. This last method is faster than bottle

Corgi puppies are born with drop ears; the speed at which they go up varies from puppy to puppy. (Photo by Winter/Churchill)

feeding but takes some practice. You must be careful that the tube goes into the stomach and not into the lungs, and, the length of the tube must be correct. And, of course, the length will change as the puppy grows. Have your veterinarian or an experienced breeder show you.

If you are tube feeding, then that probably means that the puppies are not with their dam, which means that ou have to do more than just feed them. A mother's rough cleaning with her tongue stimulates young puppies to urinate and defecate. Use a moist cotton ball and gently massage the pup's anal area after each meal.

Puppies can have problems, too, from colic to diarrhea. Sometimes the list seems so long, it is a wonder anyone has the courage to breed at all. Again, if you decide to breed, read and reread the two books mentioned earlier in this chapter. They give detailed descriptions of what can go wrong and what, if anything, you can do about it.

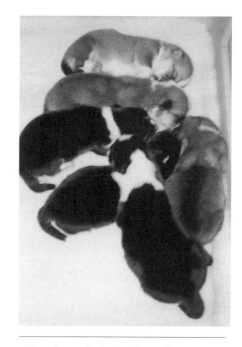

Note the undocked tails in these very young puppies. (Photo by Irma Hilts)

BASIC NEW PUPPY CARE

Assuming that all is well, tails and dewclaws should be removed at three to five days, depending on the size and health of the puppies. Most serious breeders who have been into Corgis for years will band the tails themselves, using small rubber bands tied tightly at the base of the tail to cut off circulation. Within three to five days, the tail drops off, leaving a short, clean dock. Many vets feel that banding is barbaric, however, and may lead to tetanus. Surgical docking involves less chance for infection, less pain,

a quicker procedure. One problem with having a veterinarian dock the tails, of course, is that unless that doctor knows Corgis, he could be likely to not dock the tails short enough. In my case, I felt that I was too inexperienced to try banding, but I was lucky to have a Corgi breeder for a veterinarian, so all the puppies were bundled off on day three for tails and dew claws. They screamed quite hardily for a moment and then totally forgot about it.

Unless you have an experienced breeder working with you, I'd advise having your veterinarian do the job. Having said that, make sure that your

These four puppies are trying "real" food. (Photo by Susan Ewing)

veterinarian understands just how short Corgi tails should be docked. My Heather's tail was not really properly done; the veterinarian who docked hers didn't understand how to do it correctly.

ADVANCED PUPPY CARE

Once the puppies' eyes have opened and they are crawling around, they can be moved to a larger area. Line the floor with plastic and then newspaper, and use a piece of indoor-outdoor carpet to provide better footing for the puppies. If you can get the end rolls of newsprint from your local newspaper, use that instead of newspaper; it prevents the "tattle-tale gray" that your puppies will get from the ink of a newspaper. Also, the end rolls give you larger continuous sheets of paper.

Corgi puppies are born with drop ears, and the speed with which they go up varies from puppy to puppy. Frequently, they go up and down all through teething. My first puppy came home at 8 weeks with both ears up, but whenever the weather was humid, one ear drooped. My latest pup came home with one very soft, slightly floppy ear, and it took until she was about 7 months old before it decided to stay up. If it makes you nervous, you can tape the ear with wide masking tape. Just never leave the tape on longer than three days, which is about how long the sticky part of the tape stays sticky anyway.

Weaning puppies takes place at three to four weeks. I fed mine on a slurry of blender-ground puppy food, liver, condensed milk, yogurt, baby vitamin drops and eggs, gradually reducing the liquid portions until they were eating moistened kibble and, finally, dry kibble. I fed them from a communal pan, but there were only four of them. For larger litters, you might want to feed in smaller groups or individually to make sure that all are getting their fair share.

FINDING GOOD HOMES FOR THE PUPPIES

Finally, with help from breeders, friends, veterinarians and authors, you've produced healthy Corgi puppies that are ready for a family of their own. You've come full circle, and now you are the breeder searching for the family that is just right for your "perfect" baby.

Don't forget what you learned when you were looking for a puppy. Ask prospective buyers who will be the primary caregiver, and ask how the puppy will be exercised. Does the family have a fenced yard? Will they take the puppy for frequent walks on its lead? How many children are in the family? How old are they? Is the puppy to be a companion for the children? If so, ask some questions about how the children will be taught to treat the dog. If possible, have the entire family see the puppies. Watch how each family member handles and treats the puppies. Create a contract and spell out expectations regarding showing, if any, and spaying and neutering. You have produced this puppy, and you are responsible for its well-being.

Send your puppy out into the world with a clear health record, his favorite toy and, most importantly, your phone number.

Thirteen-year-old Lamin Berenstain's Bear and fifteen-year-old Lamin Temptation. (Photo by A-N PRODUCTIONS/Tom and Linda Nutting)

CHAPTER 13

The Older Pembroke Welsh Corgi

Older dogs can be a real delight. They are familiar with what you want, and they make no demands as far as training goes. They don't need to be taught English, the way a puppy does. They are content to snooze the evening away if you are watching television, and, if you have an early evening, that's fine with them. They'll sleep in, too.

But, you have to remember that senior dogs are indeed getting older. Be aware of their age, and treat them accordingly. They will still enjoy walks, but they will tire more quickly, so you may have to shorten the walk or take it at a slower pace. The game of fetch they've always enjoyed may also have to be shortened. If your dog was used to traveling with you to events, make a point to still take the dog with you somewhere. Just because older dogs can't do what they did when they were young doesn't mean that they don't want to still be included. They will have a happier old age if they can be with you.

Being older doesn't have to mean retirement. Jason (Am./Can. Ch. Blaizewood Hooray Henry, CDX) is shown here at age 11, with his 8-year-old son, Ch. Ariel's Cullum Kill, CDX. (Photo by Bernard Kernan)

HEALTH CONCERNS FOR THE OLDER DOG

Senility, or cognitive dysfunction, may afflict an older animal. You may notice that your dog sleeps days and is restless at night. Another common indicator is that the dog will stand at the wrong side of a door, at the hinge side instead of the side that opens. He also might not want as much affection. Fortunately, drugs are now available to help make the dogs more aware and able to enjoy their life more. It's very important that you be aware that this is normal aging behavior and that you don't get annoyed with a dog in this condition. Remember what the dog gave you in his youth,

and protect and coddle him in return. If you are too busy and are likely to be irritated with such a dog, maybe it's time to think about euthanasia.

While your dog may appear just as healthy and active as ever, when he reaches the age of 8, it is a good idea to have a chemical blood screen test done at least once a year. A geriatric profile done early may alert you and your vet to a problem, or pinpoint when a specific problem started. Have your dog's thyroid checked every year or two as well. Thyroid problems are not more common in Corgis than in any other breed, but this can be a problem that's sometimes overlooked. Also monitor your dog's weight. Any unexplained weight loss is always a matter for concern. In addition, older dogs are apt to get arthritis, and extra weight can aggravate the condition. Take care of your dog's teeth always, but be especially vigilant with an older dog—he may not be able to fight off an infection as easily as a younger dog.

Some veterinarians feel that aging Corgis seem to be at risk for spleenic tumors. Veterinarian Lucy Jones speculates that herding breeds might be more prone to this problem because the tumors appear with some frequency in both German Shepherd Dogs and Corgis. Spleenic tumors are the most common cause of anemia in older dogs, and the tumors are frequently cancerous. Kidney problems, with the resultant loss of bladder control, are one of the main reasons for euthanasia, as is cancer, which is also very common in older dogs.

Remember what your dog gave you in his youth, and coddle him in his golden years. This is Jason at 12 years of age. (Photo by Ariel Corgis)

Quality endures: Look at Ch. Tri-umph's Turning Heads, CD, NA ("Shirley"), who won the PWCCA National Specialty in 1989 at age 2 . . . (Photo by Vahaly)

Veterinarians commonly recommend senior dog foods, especially Hills Science Diet and Purina brands, because they are easier on the kidneys. Veterinarian William Seleen also says that although he doesn't recommend supplements generally, B-vitamins are a good addition to the diet if the dog is urinating and drinking excessively. Also add a multivitamin for older Corgis because they put on weight so easily on a fairly small amount of food that they may not get enough food to give them the vitamins they need.

Each dog is an individual, so watch for changes and discuss them with your vet. Early detection of any condition will increase the odds that you will continue to enjoy your dog's company.

. . . and competed in the 1999 PWCCA National Specialty, ten years later at age 12. (Photo by Susan Ewing)

This is not to say that after your dog turns 8, there's nothing else you can do with your dog. Ch. Tri-umph's Turning Heads, CD, NA, who was best of breed at the PWCCA National Specialty in 1989 at the age of 2, got her Novice Agility title in 1999 at the age of 12! She also placed fourth in the Veteran's class at the PWCCA National Specialty in September 1999, and owner Marian Johnson Your is now training her for a Companion Dog Excellent (CDX) title. Take a look at the picture of Jason (Am./Can. Ch. Blaizewood Hooray Henry CDX) at age 11, with his 8-year old son, Ch. Ariel's Cullum Kill, CDX. Corgis are fantastic dogs—with proper care, you and the dog should be able to enjoy his senior years. Just be aware that they *are* the senior years, and be alert to possible health problems.

WHEN THE END IS NEAR

Eventually, no matter how well you care for your dog, he will reach the end of his allotted life span. For Corgis, that seems to be around 14 years, although some Corgis have lived into their late teens.

Some dogs die in their sleep, but most do not. Most dogs' lives today are ended by euthanasia. This is one of the hardest decisions that you will ever make concerning your dog, but it also can be one of the kindest. You have it in your power to end suffering and, in many cases, a slow, wasting death.

If It Should Be

If it should be that I grow frail and weak
And pain should keep me from my sleep
Then you must do what must be done
For this, the last battle can't be won.
You will be sad, I understand
Don't let your grief then stay your hand,
For this day, more than the rest,
Your love and friendship stand the test.
We've had so many happy years,
What is to come can hold no fears.
You'd not want me to suffer so,
When the time comes, please let me go.
Take me where my needs they'll tend
Only, stay with me to the end
And hold me firm and speak to me
Until my eyes no longer see.
I know in time that you will see
It is a kindness you do to me
Although my tail its last has waved,
From pain and suffering, I've been saved.
Don't grieve that it should be you
Who has to decide this thing to do.
We've been so close, we two these years
Don't let your heart hold any tears.

—Reprinted from Our Corgi World, *1995, with permission of The Welsh Corgi League, England. Author unknown.*

Most veterinarians use an overdose of the anesthetic pentobarbitol for euthanasia. The process is fast and painless. Some people can't bear to be with their dog at the time of death, while others are there until the final breath. I didn't know which I would choose until the first time it happened, and then I knew for certain that I would not leave my dog's side while I could still offer any comfort at all. Each time I've held back my tears until it is over because all my Corgis have been sensitive to my tears, and I don't want to add any more stress. I just pet them and tell them that they are good dogs.

The day I took my first Corgi, Brecon, to the vet to be euthanized, I carried along two hot dogs and three chocolate bars, which I fed him just before the needle found the vein. Since then, illness has made the various dogs disinterested in food, so that was the first and only time I ever did that. Brecon was such a chow hound that it comforts me to remember him wolfing down the treats.

Talk to your veterinarian beforehand about how the clinic disposes of the body. Many vets offer cremation and will return the ashes to you if you wish. Some have their own crematory on the premises; others send the bodies away. Whatever your decision, if you decide to bury your dog yourself, check with local health regulations. Finally, what you hold in your mind and your heart is more important than where the dog's remains lie:

For if the dog be well remembered, if sometimes she leaps through your dreams actual as in life, eyes kindling, laughing, begging, it matters not where that dog sleeps. On a hill where the wind is unrebuked and the trees are roaring, or beside a stream she knew in puppyhood, or somewhere in the flatness of a pastureland where most exhilarating cattle graze. It is one to a dog, and all one to you, and nothing is gained and nothing lost—if memory lives. But there is one best place to bury a dog.

If you bury her in this spot, she will come to you when you call—come to you over the grim, dim frontiers of death, and down the well-remembered path and to your side again. And though you may call a dozen living dogs to heel, they shall not growl at her nor resent her coming, for she belongs there.

People may scoff at you, who see no lightest blade of grass bend by her footfall, who hear no whimper, people who have never really had a dog. Smile at them, for you shall know something that is hidden from them.

The one best place to bury a good dog is in the heart of her master . . .

—*Ben Hur Lampman*
The Oregonian, *1925*

Am./Can. Ch. Llanelly's Carillon. (Photo by Lucy E. Jones, DVM)

CHAPTER 14

The Pembroke Welsh Corgi Club of America

As frequently happens with any group of like-minded people, Corgi fanciers in both Britain and the United States got together to form clubs dedicated to preserving the dogs they loved.

The first such club was formed in 1925 and was called simply The Corgi Club. Later the word "Welsh" was added, making it the Welsh Corgi Club. This early club began in Carmarthen, Wales, and included both Cardigan and Pembroke Welsh Corgi fanciers.

THE WELSH CORGI LEAGUE

Passion for the Corgi was not limited to Wales. The breed became popular in England, and gradually Corgis were able to compete for Challenge Certificates offered at many shows. In June 1938, with the encouragement of Mrs. Thelma Gray of Rozavel Kennels, the Welsh Corgi League was formed. Its membership is open to Corgi fanciers all over the world, and its annual publication, the *Welsh Corgi League Handbook* is appreciated by all. First published in 1946 under editor Edith Osborne, the *Handbook* is distributed free to all members, and it is the model for similar volumes in other countries. In this country, the

Pembroke Welsh Corgi Club of America publishes an annual handbook that offers similar information on Corgis who have won titles, as well as health tips, human interest stories and how-to articles.

The Welsh Corgi League also made the first documentary on the breed, a 25-minute color film, *Corgwn Sir Bonfire*.

Many smaller groups of Corgi lovers also exist in Britain, and a complete list is available from the Welsh Corgi League.

THE PEMBROKE WELSH CORGI CLUB OF AMERICA, INC.

As in Britain, it didn't take long for Corgi breeders and admirers to unite in the United States.

The first Welsh Corgi Club included both Cardigan and Pembroke lovers. The Pembroke Welsh Corgi Club of America came into being on February 12, 1936, during the Westminster Kennel Club show.

The first standard for the Pembroke Welsh Corgi was short—only 120 words—and was written by the Welsh Corgi Club in 1925 and adopted by the PWCCA and approved by the American Kennel Club in March 1936.

In 1951 the PWCCA adopted the English standard for the Pembroke Welsh Corgi, with a few changes and for more than 50 years this remained the official standard of the breed. A new revised standard for Pembroke Welsh Corgis in the United States was approved by the AKC in 1972. The for mat was revised in 1993 to meet the AKC's request for uniformity between all breed standards.

Meetings were first held each year in New York during the dates of the Westminster Kennel Club dog show, although during World War II these meetings were suspended. Currently, the PWCCA holds a meeting in the fall during the National Specialty and another in the spring during a regional club specialty.

The PWCCA has a quarterly *Pembroke Welsh Corgi Newsletter*, which includes news from affiliate clubs as well as information on current Corgi wins in the show ring and interesting stories about Corgis and their owners. People interested in Corgis may write for a brochure about Corgis, and the club also produces an illustrated standard. A flyer produced by the club is sent through the AKC to each person who registers a Pembroke Welsh Corgi with it. There is also the annual handbook mentioned earlier.

Besides acting as an information center, the PWCCA sponsors the National Specialty show. The National, which rotates each year to different sections of the country, offers an entire week of Corgi fun. Besides regular conformation and obedience classes, there are sweepstakes classes for young Corgis 6 months to 18 months; Veteran's classes in both conformation and obedience, for dogs older than 8 years; team obedience; agility; and herding. Other extras may include tests for the CGC (Canine Good Citizen) award and certification as a therapy dog. The National is also the place to buy anything and everything that is Corgi-related!

PWCCA Affiliate Clubs

The requirements for membership in the PWCCA are listed in detail in Appendix B, along with the club's code of ethics. Regional affiliate clubs, which have their own membership guidelines and hold their own annual specialties, are listed in Appendix A.

Besides the benefits of the publications produced by regional clubs and the national club, belonging to a Corgi club puts you in touch with other like-minded people. Club mailing lists make it easy to contact other Corgi owners for information and advice. Being on a club mailing list also means that you will receive information on specialty shows, agility trials, obedience competition, herding tests and tracking seminars. Joining a club is a great way to keep in touch with the world of the Corgi.

Appendix A

Resources

The following list of Corgi clubs and dog-related organizations will help you obtain any information you seek regarding Corgis. Club contacts and addresses may change, but the parent club will always have updated information. For updated parent club information, contact the AKC.

Organizations

AKC Gazette Editorial Offices
260 Madison Ave.
New York, NY 10017
212-696-8390

American Kennel Club
5580 Centerview Dr.
Suite 200
Raleigh, NC 27606-3390
919-233-9767

American Kennel Club Library
260 Madison Ave.
New York, NY 10017
212-696-8245

North American Dog Agility Council
HCR 2, Box 277
St. Maries, ID 83861

Therapy Dogs International
6 Hilltop Rd.
Mendham, NJ 07945

United States Dog Agility Association
P.O. Box 850955
Richardson, TX 75085

The Pembroke Welsh Corgi
Club of America, Inc., Affiliate Clubs and Contacts (1999)

Cascade Pembroke Welsh Corgi Club, Inc.
Amanda Reinhardt
6515 229th Ave. NE
Redmond, WA 98053

Columbia River Pembroke Welsh Corgi Club
Debbie Scott
1250 NE 52nd Ave.
Portland, OR 97213

Golden Gate Pembroke Welsh Corgi Fanciers, Inc.
Kay Hammel
10621 Minnesota Ave.
Penngrove, CA 94951

Greater Houston Pembroke Welsh Corgi Fanciers
Diana Carfello
9538 Meadowbriar Lane
Houston, TX 77063

Lakeshore Pembroke Welsh Corgi Club, Inc.
Mindy Holmes
2181 Second St.
Northbrook, IL 60062

Mayflower Pembroke Welsh Corgi Club, Inc.
Dolores Bechard
68 Laurie Lane
Lowell, MA 01854

North Texas Pembroke Welsh Corgi Fanciers
Robyn Finley
5009 South Dr.
Fort Worth, TX 76132

Ohio Valley Pembroke Welsh Corgi Club
Sandra Combs
8099 E. Factory Rd. W
Alexandria, OH 45381

Pembroke Welsh Corgi Club of the Garden State, Inc.
Doris McGee
126 Marsh Circle, Woodsville Rd.
Hopewell, NJ 08525

Pembroke Welsh Corgi Club of Greater Atlanta, Inc.
Jody Allgood
4315 Garmon Rd.
Atlanta, GA 30327

Pembroke Welsh Corgi Club of the Potomac
Kathryn O'Bryant
P.O. Box 339
Wakefield, VA 23888

Pembroke Welsh Corgi Club of Southern California, Inc.
Gwen Platt
860 Leah Lane
Escondido, CA 92029

Sunshine Pembroke Welsh Corgi Club, Inc.
Fran Gammie
810 NE 118th St.
Biscayne Park, FL 33161

(Photo by Winter/Churchill)

Pembroke Welsh Corgi Club of America, Inc., Code of Ethics

REQUIREMENTS FOR MEMBERSHIP

Listed below are the requirements for membership into the PWCCA and the club's code of ethics. Under the requirements for membership, number 3, a "worker" is anyone who works during a show presented by his club. A club member may steward (help the judge in the ring), be obedience chair, show chair, trophy chair, work on publicity or hospitality or be in charge of finding a place for the show and hiring tents. There's always something to do at a show!

The code of ethics was developed by the PWCCA as the standard of behavior for a responsible breeder and/or Corgi owner. It was developed to help ensure proper breeding practices and quality living conditions for the Pembroke Welsh Corgi.

1. Must be an owner of Pembroke Welsh Corgis for a minimum of four years

2. Must be a member of a Pembroke Welsh Corgi Club or a local all-breed or obedience club for a minimum of three years

3. Must have meaningful experience as an exhibitor, a breeder and/or a club member, and a worker for a minimum of three years

4. Must demonstrate adherence to the breeding and selling practices described in the PWCCA Code of Ethics

5. Must exhibit good sportsmanship in all phases of dog activities

6. Must be sponsored by two current PWCCA members who have known the candidate for a minimum of two years.

CODE OF ETHICS

1. All Pembroke Welsh Corgi Club of America (PWCCA) members and affiliate clubs shall be dedicated to the preservation and welfare of the Pembroke Welsh Corgi breed.

2. All PWCCA members and affiliate clubs must ensure that their actions are in the best interest of the breed, this club, and its members.

3. The prime objective for breeding the Pembroke Welsh Corgi is to produce animals of exceptional quality.

A. Only dogs and bitches of sound temperament and structure, good health, and characteristic type as described in the American Kennel Club's (AKC) approved Official Standard for the Pembroke Welsh Corgi should be used for breeding.

B. Dogs and bitches should not be used for further breeding if they have, in two litters, produced offspring with the same serious genetic defect such as: blindness, deafness, lameness, or impairment of vital functions which prevent these offspring from living a normal, healthy life without major surgical or significant medical intervention.

C. Bitches to be bred must be in robust health. Eyes and hips should be checked and found to be within normal limits. A bitch is not to be bred prior to one year of age or older than eight years, nor should she produce more than six litters in her lifetime. A bitch should not be bred more than two out of three consecutive seasons.

D. Stud service should be offered only to bitches whose owners adhere to the above guidelines.

E. A male should not be used at stud unless his hips and eyes are checked and found to be within normal limits.

F. Members should not consider breeding a litter unless they are prepared to keep the resultant puppies for as long as it takes to suitably place each puppy. Members offering stud service should request the above assurance from the owners of bitches.

G. Members should take lifetime responsibility to ensure that Pembrokes of their breeding are cared for in a safe and healthy environment.

H. The breeder of a rescued Pembroke, who is a member of PWCCA shall, upon notification, provide for the Corgi's care.

4. The selling of puppies and adult Pembrokes must be accomplished in a manner that reflects the PWCCA member's care, concern and integrity.

A. All puppies and adults shall be maintained and/or sold in a clean and healthy condition.

B. Puppies are to be a minimum of eight weeks old, have received the appropriate vaccination and worming, and should be examined by a veterinarian prior to sale.

C. A spay/neuter contract shall be used in the sale of a puppy or adult showing a very serious fault as described in the Standard or other faults such as monorchidism or cryptorchidism. Members are encouraged to use the limited registration option offered by the American Kennel Club.

D. Written agreements are recommended to specify details of the sale including health guarantees and the breeder's lifetime responsibility. The purchaser shall be provided with accurate and valid documentation of the Pembroke's AKC registration and pedigree.

E. There must be no wholesaling of litters or selling of breeding stock to pet dealers, commercial retailers or distributors or to any party for the purpose of resale. No member should be associated with an auction, lottery, or raffle involving dogs for the prize.

5. Good sportsmanship is essential for all PWCCA members.

A. All members shall conduct themselves in a manner that reflects credit on the Pembroke Welsh Corgi and the PWCCA.

B. Members should not engage in false or misleading advertising or other misrepresentation of the Pembroke(s).

C. Members should not make false or misleading statements regarding their competitor's person, Pembroke or breeding practices.

D. Members shall be accountable for the actions of an employed handler as they pertain to the Code of Ethics.

(Photo by Gail Painter)

Titles a Corgi Can Earn

AVAILABLE TITLES, PWCCA AWARDS AND KEY TO AWARD ABBREVIATIONS

AKC Championship titles always precede a dog's name:

Ch.—Conformation Champion
OTCH—Obedience Trial Champion
H. Ch.—Herding Champion
C.T.—Champion Tracker
MACH—Master Agility Champion

Titles for AKC Obedience and other performance events always follow a dog's name:

CD—Companion Dog
CDX—Companion Dog Excellent
UD—Utility Dog
UDX—Utility Dog Excellent

TD—Tracking Dog

TDX—Tracking Dog Excellent
VST—Variable Surface Tracking Test

NA—Novice Agility
OA—Open Agility
AX—Agility Excellent
MX—Master Agility Excellent

NAJ—Novice JWW (Jumper with Weaves)
OAJ—Open JWW
AXJ—Excellent JWW
MXJ—Master Excellent JWW

HS—Herding Started
HI—Herding Intermediate
HX—Herding Excellent

Special titles appear after a dog's name:

A Canine Good Citizen (CGC) title is administered by the AKC.

Dogs can attain Therapy Dog status through several Therapy Dog organizations.

PWCCA titles always follow a dog's name:

ROM—Register of Merit
ROMX—Register of Merit Excellent
VC—Versatile Corgi
VCX—Versatile Corgi Excellent

At the September 1990 meeting of the Pembroke Welsh Corgi Club of America, the Board of Directors approved the establishment of a Register of Merit (ROM) and Register of Merit Excellent (ROMX) for those dogs meeting the requirements. It is not necessary to belong to the PWCCA to qualify; this award is given at the annual meeting. ROM for males requires 10 Champions sired; for bitches, 5 Champions must be produced. ROMX for males requires 15 Champions sired; for bitches, 8 Champions must be produced.

PEMBROKE WELSH CORGI CLUB OF AMERICA, INC., REGISTER OF MERIT (ROM) LIST

These dogs have attained the Register of Merit (ROM) ranking from the PWCCA, as of December 31, 1998:

Ch. Adastars Good Golly Ms. Dolly, ROM
Ch. Albelarm Superstar of Fox Run, ROM
Ch. Amsburg's Own Phat Albert, ROM
Apple Taffy of Furnace Brook, ROM
Ch. Arbor Festiniog Idle Gossip, ROM
Ch. Arbor's Esther, ROM
Ch. Athwin Magic Flute, ROM
Ch. Baccarat of Chryndom, ROM
Ch. Bear Acres Mister Snowshoes, UD, ROM
Ch. Bear Acres Two For The Road, ROM
Ch. Beckridge Amanda of Pemlea, ROM
Ch. Benfro Abigail Adams, ROM
Ch. Benfro Eloise, ROM
Ch. Bicliff's Token Motion, ROM
Ch. Blaizewood Hooray Henry, CDX, ROM
Ch. Blujor Dickens Desert Fox, ROM
Ch. Blujor Ensemble, CD, ROM
Ch. Blujor Winsome Lass, CD, ROM
Ch. Bowman Benita, ROM
Ch. Bridholme Jordanian Sunlight, ROM
Ch. Brookehaven Sweet Serenade, ROM
Ch. Brynlea Royalfox Show Stopper, ROM
Ch. Busy B's Bark of Ammanford, ROM
Ch. Busy B's Sweet Dreams, ROM
Ch. Caralon's Lana Lee, ROM
Caralon's Punky Brewster, ROM

Ch. Caralon's Q-S Hot Wheels, ROM

Ch. Caralon's Tegwyn Sian, CDX, HC, TT, ROM

Ch. Champagne N Caviar, ROM

Ch. Citadel Barbican, ROM

Ch. Clayview's Dainty Maid, ROM

Ch. Corgard's I Deliver Em', ROM

Ch. Cormanby Coppersmith, ROM

Ch. Cormanby Pert Princess, ROM

Ch. Cote de Neige Bear Acres Coins, ROM

Ch. Cote de Neige Christmas Rush, ROM

Cote de Neige Clarinet, ROM

Ch. Cote de Neige Fairy Tale, ROM

Ch. Cote de Neige Fortune Cookie, ROM

Ch. Cote de Neige Garland, ROM

Ch. Cote de Neige High Tea, ROM

Ch. Cote de Neige Magic Flute, ROM

Ch. Cote de Neige Necklace, ROM

Cote de Neige Pat-A-Cake, ROM

Ch. Cote de Neige Red Cherry, ROM

Ch. Cote de Neige Red Rattle, ROM

Ch. Cote de Neige Rush Hour, ROM

Cote de Neige Sea Shell, ROM

Ch. Cote de Neige Show Piece, ROM

Ch. Crawleycrow Coracle of Aimhi, ROM

Ch. Craythornes Cassia of Cowfold, ROM

Ch. Crowleythorn Ladomoorlands, ROM

Crysmont's Roebling Opal, ROM

Ch. Cypress Astoria, ROM

Cypress Delta Dawn, ROM

Ehrstag's Betsy, ROM

Ch. Elfwish Pea Pod Pixie. ROM

Ch. Emlyn's Executive, ROM

Ch. Eversridge Firebird, ROM

Ch. Far Away Honey Candy, ROM

Fenlea Special Moonshine, ROM

Ch. Festiniog's Toby Two, ROM

Ch. Fire Bird of Cogges, ROM

Ch. Fitzdown Salmon Spray, ROM

Ch. Fourwents Brondda of Andely, ROM

Ch. Fox Meadows Shasta, HC, ROM

Foxtale's Good News Bear, ROM

Foxway Marnac Ali-Oops, ROM

Garvin's Covey Rise, ROM

Ch. Grand Cayman of Chryndom, ROM

Greenforest's Diedra, ROM

Ch. Halmor Hi-Fi, ROM

Ch. Halmor's Winrod Spencer, ROM

Ch. Heronsway Mata Hari, ROM

Ch. Hildenmanor Magenta, ROM

Ch. Honeyfox Starstruck, ROM

Ch. Jade Tree Just Deserts, ROM

Ch. Jade Tree Penway Up Country, HC, ROM

Ch. Kamiri Magic Connection, ROM

Ch. Kamiri Midnite Bliss, ROM

Karolaska Chinkapin, ROM

Katydid's Bronz M'Jammey, ROM

Ch. Katydid's Ebonsu Molly, ROM

Ch. Katydid's Sunny K'Phar Lap, CDX, TDX, ROM

Ch. Kaydon Eversridge Penny, ROM

Ch. Kaydon's Sue, CD, ROM

Ch. Kempio's I'm An Angel, ROM

Ch. Kennadale's Chloe, ROM

Ch. Lamin Rumor Has It, ROM

Ch. Larchmont's Ali'Se, ROM

Ch. Larchmont's Buff Puff, ROM

Ch. Larchmont's Cream Puff, ROM

Ch. Larchmont's Diamond Buffer, ROM

Ch. Larchmont's Linvar Candyman, HC, ROM

Ch. Larklain Babeta, ROM
Ch. Larklain Bandits Dart, ROM
Ch. Larklain-Bj Legends Sunshine, ROM
Larklain Stoneys Gigget, HC, ROM
Larklain's Butter Fox, ROM
Ch. Larklain's Dandy Ambassador, ROM
Ch. Larklain's Dandy Sunsprite, ROM
Ch. Larklain's Empress, ROM
Ch. Larklain's Firebright, ROM
Ch. Larklain's Funtime Stardust, ROM
Larklain's Master Cameo, ROM
Larklain's Token, ROM
Ch. Larklain's Toppy, ROM
Ch. Lees Craythorne's Golden Plover, ROM
Lees Lizette, ROM
Ch. Lees Mynah, CD, TD, ROM
Ch. Left Bank Valedictorian, ROM
Ch. Lin-Kel's I'm No Hooker, ROM
Linvar's Rockin Robyn, ROM
Ch. Llanfair Bright Promise, CD, ROM
Ch. Lonikii's Domino Intowishin, ROM
Ch. Lonikii's Raisin' Cane, ROM
Ch. M-Candol Betcha Babe, ROM
Ch. M-Candol's Rochill Fergie, ROM
Ch. Macksons The Young Pretender, ROM
Ch. Maracas Gale Force of Cleden, ROM
Ch. Marlou Imagination, ROM
Ch. Master Major of Millerhof, ROM
Ch. Megan of Karenhurst, ROM
Ch. Menfreyas Classical Jazz, ROM
Ch. My Gay Charmer, CD, ROM
Ch. Nebriowa Amber Mist, ROM
Ch. Nebriowa Giorgio, ROM
Ch. Nebriowa Image of Rosewood, ROM

Ch. Nebriowa Stitch In Time, ROM
Ch. Nebriowa Weatherstone Spree, ROM
Northwood M-Tak Penneystock, CDX, ROM, CGC
Ch. Northwood Spellbound, ROM
O'Melaghlin's Mistytoo, ROM
Omega's Illusion, ROM
Ch. Parisien Model, ROM
Ch. Peggysmill Smart Guy, ROM
Ch. Pemland Maestro, ROM
Ch. Pemland Symphony, ROM
Pemlea's Classy Affair, ROM
Ch. Penmoel Mitzi, ROM
Ch. Pennington Benchmark, ROM
Ch. Pennington Glory Hallelujah, ROM
Ch. Penrick Flewellyn, CD, ROM
Penway's Silver Silhouette, ROM
Ch. Pettiwood's Superman, ROM
Ch. Pinemeade Garden Party, ROM
Ch. Popplebury High Blaze, ROM
Ch. Presqu'Ile Llani, ROM
Ch. Quandas Buffy Saint Marie, ROM
Ch. Renefield Sport Coat, ROM
Ch. Revelmere In The Pink, ROM
Ch. Riverside Dream Addition, UDT, HE, VC, ROM
Ch. Rivona Moon Melody, ROM
Ch. Rock Creek Somerset Magnolia, TD, ROM
Ch. Roughouse Applause Applause, CDX, TD, ROM
Ch. Roughouse Pennington Daryl, ROM
Roughouse Standing Ovation, ROM
Rover Run Ojai Bell, ROM
Rover Run Romance, ROM
Ch. Rowell Fine Finish, ROM
Ch. Rozavel Uncle Sam of Waseeka, ROM
Ch. Rryde Symphony, ROM

Ch. Schaferhaus Aeroglend Tupnc, ROM
Ch. Schaferhaus Danielle, ROM
Ch. Schaferhaus Fogcutter, UD, HC, PT, ROM
Schaferhaus Honey N'Cream, ROM
Schaferhaus Supersmooch, ROM
Ch. Scotmorns Designer Genes, HC, ROM
Ch. Shavals Fire Master, ROM
Ch. Sippiwisset Compass Rose, ROM
Ch. Snowdonia's Black Knight, ROM
Ch. Snowdonia's Duplicate Copy, ROM
Ch. Snowdonia's Four Roses, ROM
Ch. Spartan of Blands of Werwow, ROM
Ch. Stokeplain Fair Chance Cote de Neige, ROM
Ch. Stormerbanks Poetry, ROM
Stormerbanks Timbermist, ROM
Ch. Stormwey Paddy, ROM
Ch. Sunny Bank's Windjammer Tart, CD, ROM
Ch. Tams Jazzman of Larchmont, ROM
Ch. Tandem Acres Cinnamon Toast, ROM
Ch. Tegwen of Chryndom, ROM
Ch. Terenelf's Honeyfox, ROM
Terenelf's Tickle My Fancy, ROM
Ch. Thompson's Tom-Foolery, ROM
Ch. Trewhyl Lyric of Pennington, ROM
Ch. Triad Toast of the Town, CD, HC, ROM
Ch. Ursa Major Daemon Keshlorian, ROM
Ch. Velour of Rowell, ROM
Ch. Vennwood's Masterpiece, ROM
Ch. Virginia of Fox Covert, ROM
Ch. Walborah Xie Xie of Renefield, ROM
Ch. Walborah's Hobby, ROM
Waseeka's Topaz, ROM
Ch. Wee Folks Tudor Tapestry, HC, ROM
Ch. Welcanis Constellation Faraway, ROM

Ch. Wicklow's Whizzer, ROM
Ch. Willets Red Jacket, ROM
Wyeford Bonny Madam, ROM
Ch. Zorro Miel of Menfreya, ROM

PEMBROKE WELSH CORGI CLUB OF AMERICA, INC., REGISTER OF MERIT EXCELLENT (ROMX) LIST

As of December 31, 1998, the following dogs have acquired the Register of Merit Excellent (ROMX) rank from the PWCCA:

Ch. Anzil Elegant Lady, ROMX
Ch. Beaujolais of Revelmere, ROMX
Ch. Bekonpenn Count Doronicum CD, ROMX
Ch. Belroyd Seabird, ROMX
Ch. Benfro Lord Gambier, ROMX
Ch. Braxentra Michaelmas, ROMX
Ch. Brookehaven Pfief And Drum, HC, ROMX
Ch. Busy B's Cherry Bark Key, ROMX
Ch. Cadno Melanie, ROMX
Ch. Cappykorns Bach, ROMX
Ch. Caralon's Q-T Sequoya, ROMX
Ch. Clayfield Paisley, ROMX
Ch. Cormanby Cavalier, ROMX
Ch. Cote de Neige Chance of Fox Run, ROMX
Ch. Cote de Neige Christmas Candy, ROMX
Ch. Cote de Neige Instant Replay, ROMX
Ch. Cote de Neige Pennysaver, ROMX
Ch. Cote de Neige Sundew, ROMX
Ch. Courtllyn Chagal, ROMX
Ch. Faraway The Magic Kan-D-Kid, CD, ROMX

Ch. Festiniog's Moonraker, ROMX

Ch. Festiniog's Touchdown, UDX, PT, NA, ROMX, VC

Ch. Foxash Dawn Piper of Rowell, ROMX

Ch. Garvin's Magic Marker, ROMX

Ch. Gaylord's Bobbindobber, ROMX

Ch. Halmor Pathfinder, ROMX

Ch. Heronsway Freestyle, UDT, HT, TT, VC, ROMX

Ch. Hildenmanor Master Spy, ROMX

Ch. Honeyfox Starstruck, ROMX

Ch. Horoko Caralon Dickens, ROMX, CGC

Ch. Irisan Bengimum Boy of Rivona, CD, ROMX

Ch. Larchmont's Golden Triumph, CD, ROMX

Ch. Larklain Bandits Red Sun, ROMX

Ch. Larklain Topper, ROMX

Ch. Larklain's Master Dare, ROMX

Ch. Larklain's Redd Dandy, ROMX

Ch. Lees Briardale Midnight, ROMX

Ch. Lees Symphony, ROMX

Ch. Leonine Leprechaun, ROMX

Ch. Lynfarne Poldark, ROMX

Ch. M-Candol E-Z Todoittoo, CD, CGC, ROMX

Ch. Magnum of Vennwoods, ROMX

Ch. Mar-Wil's Cayenne Pepper, ROMX

Ch. Maracas Monarch of Cleden, ROMX

Ch. Martindale Butter Brickle, ROMX

Ch. Nebriowa Christian Dior, ROMX

Ch. Nebriowa Front and Center, ROMX

Ch. Nebriowa Greenforest Ranger, ROMX

Ch. Nebriowa Jordache Fox Meadow, ROMX

Ch. Nebriowa Jovan, ROMX

Ch. Nebriowa The Blacksmith, DCX, ROMX

Ch. Nebriowa Vangard Center Line, ROMX

Ch. Northwoods Song and Dance, ROMX

Ch. Otreks Herman Josephs, ROMX

Ch. Pennington Ramblin' Lad, ROMX

Ch. Penway's Town And Country, ROMX

Ch. Pinemeade Paper Dragon, ROMX

Ch. Red Envoy of Brome, CD, ROMX

Ch. Revelmere Bring Me Joy, ROMX

Ch. Rivona Such Success, ROMX

Ch. Rivona Top Notch, ROMX

Ch. Rupertbear of Wey, ROMX

Ch. Schaferhaus Usherhaus Robbi, ROMX

Ch. Schaferhaus Yul B of Quanda, ROMX

Ch. Shavals Fire Master, ROMX

Ch. Stormerbanks Tristram of Cote de Neige, ROMX

Ch. Stormerbanks Winrod Fergus, ROMX

Ch. Suzyque's Southern Snowbear, ROMX

Ch. Triad Captain Crunch, CDX, OA, HC, CGC, ROMX

Ch. Tymawr Roamer, ROMX

Ch. Vangard Mister Ski Bum, ROMX

Ch. Vangard The Last Chance, ROMX

Ch. Vennwoods Zodiac, ROMX

National Specialty Winners

Note: No National Specialty show was held in 1943, 1944, and 1945; Two National Specialty shows were held in 1960 and 1963.

1999: Ch. Ninacorte For Your Eyes Only
Owners: Carol Asteris and Linda Canfield
Breeders: Haddi Kurniawan and
   Lina S. Kurniawan

1998: Ch. Hallmark's Olympian
Owners: Cynthia and Vicent Savioli, and
   Midge Ruscak
Breeder: Midge Ruscak

1997: Ch. Fox Meadows Forest Gump
Owners: Douglas Wilson, Sally Stewart Bishop,
   and Scott Yergin
Breeders: Sally Stewart Bishop and
   Scott Yergin

1996: Ch. Valhalla Heronsway Crystal
Owners: Karen and Sam Baker, and
   Anne H. Bowes
Breeders: Kathleen Liebler and Anne Bowes

1995: Ch. Jade Tree Penway Up Country
Owners: S. Lueck, M. Day, and C. Johnson
Breeders: Janice Edwards and Joan Reid

1994: Ch. Jade Tree Penway Up Country
Owners: S. Lueck, M. Day, and C. Johnson
Breeders: Janice Edwards and Joan Reid

1993: Ch. Jade Tree Penway Up Country
Owners: S. Lueck, M. Day, and C. Johnson
Breeders: Janice Edwards and Joan Reid

1992: Ch. Howbout Welsh Wonder Boy
Owners: Hill and Lonner Holden,
   and Joan Jensen
Breeders: Sally Howe and J. Steven Porter

1991: Ch. Howbout Welsh Wonder Boy
Owners: Hill and Lonner Holden,
   and Joan Jensen
Breeders: Sally Howe and J. Steven Porter

1990: Ch. Roughouse Pennington Daryl
Owners: Mr. and Mrs. Ijams, and
   Mr. and Mrs. Blakely
Breeders: Mrs. M.T. Ijams and Sue Vahaly

1989: Ch. Tri-umph's Turning Heads
Owner: Marian Johnson
Breeders: Marian Johnson and Lyn Johnson

1988: Ch. Northrun Sea-Goin' Magic
Owners: G. Ferriday and C. Donovan
Breeder: C. Donavan

1987: Ch. Nebriowa Coco Chanel
Owners: T. Mathiesen and L. Cunha
Breeders: T. Mathiesen and L. Cunha

1986: Ch. Northrun Sea-Goin' Magic
Owner: C. Donovan
Breeder: C. Donavan

1985: Ch. Trewhyl Lyric of Pennington
Owner: Shirley Brooks
Breeders: Margie Patton and Sue Vahaly

1984: Ch. Sea Masters Tigue
Owners: Randy and Marilyn Randle
Breeders: Robin Hickey and Robert Coryell

1983: Garvin's Summer Color, CDX
Owners: J. and J. Durrance, and G. Garvin

1982: Willoan's Lucky Lady
Owner: Mrs. William Kennedy
Breeder: Mrs. William Kennedy

1981: Ch. Pegasus Lori of Pennington
Owners: Sue and John Vahaly
Breeders: Mr. and Mrs. D. R. Timmons

1980: Festiniog's Moonraker
Owner: Margaret Burnett
Breeder: Margaret Thomas

1979: Ch. Busy B Sweet Cider
Owner: Lynn Brooks
Breeder: Lynn Brooks

1978: Ch. Schaferhaus Yul B of Quanda
Owners: Schaferhaus Kennels and G. A. Clarke
Breeders: Schaferhaus Kennels and G. A. Clarke

1977: Ch. Tindervale Startrek
Owner: Mrs. William B. Long
Breeder: Ms. B. Snelling

1976: Ch. Rupertbear of Wey
Owner: Mrs. Herman Bohr, Jr.
Breeder: Nan Butler

1975: Ch. Llanfair Night Owl
Owners: I. Sorley, F. Omer, and D. Christie
Breeders: Henrick and Irene Sorley

1974: Ch. Glynea Red Rose
Owner: Janet Robinson
Breeder: Charles Lewis

1973: Ch. Albelarm Superstar of Fox Run
Owner: Mrs. Alan R. Robson
Breeder: Mrs. Robert Black, Jr.

1972: Ch. Glynea Red Rose
Owner: Mrs. J. Ostrow
Breeder: Charles Lewis

1971: Velour of Rowell
Owner: Mrs. J. Ostrow
Breeder: Patrick M. Date

1970: Cote de Neige Fortune Teller
Owner: Cote de Neige Kennels
Breeder: Cote de Neige Kennels

1969: Ffondwyn Fenella of Llwynog
Owner: Mrs. R.F. Black and P. Haynam
Breeder: J. T. Williams

1968: Ch. Mackson the Young Pretender
Owner: Mrs. P. Mack
Breeder: Mrs. P. Mack

1967: Ch. Cote de Neige Pennysaver
Owner: Cote de Neige Kennels
Breeder: Cote de Neige Kennels

1966: Ch. Cote de Neige Dilly Dally
Owner: Cote de Neige Kennels
Breeder: Cote de Neige Kennels

1965: Ch. Cote de Neige Derek
Owner: Mr. and Mrs. Pillsbury
Breeder: Cote de Neige Kennels

1964: Ch. Devonshire's Deacon
Owner: Rynwood Kennels
Breeders: R. A. and Eric R. Lorgus

1963: Ch. Halmor HiFi
Owner: Mrs. E. Pimlott
Breeder: Mrs. E. Pimlott

1963: Ch. Raglan Sargent Major Justrite
Owners: J. and J. Histed
Breeders: Mr. and Mrs. Harry Dubois

1962: Ch. Willet's Red Jacket
Owner: Mrs. W. B. Long
Breeder: Dr. Matthew Ratchford

1961: Ch. Rover Run Minstrel Man
Owners: Mr. and Mrs. D. G. Rayne
Breeders: Carol Simmonds and Jack Cypress

1960: Ch. Willet's Red Jacket
Owner: Mr. W. B. Long
Breeder: Dr. Matthew Ratchford

1959: Ch. Cote de Neige Storm Cloud
Owner: Cote de Neige Kennels
Breeder: Cote de Neige Kennels

1958: Ch. Maracas Gale Force of Cleden
Owner: L. C. Cleland
Breeder: Mrs. M.T.S. Thorneycroft

1957: Ch. Macksons Coronet
Owner: Mrs. P. B. Mack
Breeder: Pamela Mack

1956: Ch. Lees Symphony
Owner: Estate of Mrs. J. D. Duncan
Breeder: Mrs. J. D. Duncan

1955: Ch. Crawleycrow Coracle of Aimhi
Owner: M. D. McCammon
Breeder: Mrs. Christopher Firbank

1954: Ch. Kaydon's Happy Talk
Owner: Mrs. J. D. Duncan
Breeder: Mrs. J. D. Duncan

1953: Ch. Lees Symphony
Owner: Mrs. J.D. Duncan
Breeder: Mrs. J. D. Duncan

1952: Ch. Rozavel Rainbow
Owner: Mrs. A. W. Porter
Breeder: Mrs. K. Robinson

1951: Hollyheath Pilot of Waseeka
Owner: Waseeka Kennels
Breeders: M. Heath and B. M. Holloway

1950: Ch. Rozavel Lucky Fellow of Merriedip
Owner: Merriedip Kennels
Breeder: F. Tomlinson

1949: Ch. Formakin Orangeman
Owner: Greencorg Kennels
Breeder: Greencorg Kennels

1948: Formakin Orangeman
Owner: Greencorg Kennels
Breeder: Greencorg Kennels

1947: Ch. Tormentor of Andely
Owner: Barbara L. Fallass
Breeder: Barbara L. Fallass

1946: Ch. Peppercorn Formakin
   Fascination of Andely
Owner: Barbara L. Fallass
Breeder: J. Holmes, Jr.

1942: Waseeka's Din
Owner: Waseeka Kennels
Breeder: Waseeka Kennels

1941: Ch. Fire Bird of Cogges
Owner: Barbara L. Fallass
Breeder: Barbara L. Fallass

1940: Ch. Lisaye Rattle
Owner: Waseeka Kennels
Breeder: D.E.M. Shepperd

1939: Ch. Fitzdown Paul of Andely
Owner: Barbara L. Fallass
Breeder: Barbara L. Fallass

1938: Rozavel Rufus of Merriedip
Owner: Mrs. Lewis Roesler
Breeder: M. Maynard

1937: Ch. Lisaye Rattle
Owner: Waseeka Kennels
Breeder: D.E.M. Shepperd

1936: Defiant Girl of Merriedip
Owner: Mrs. Lewis Roesler
Breeder: F. A. Lewis

(Photo by Winter/Churchill)

Bibliography

As a lover of books as well as dogs, I have gained great insight from this select list into dogs in general, as well as Pembroke Welsh Corgis specifically. Some of these titles may be out of print, but most still are available through a book dealer, at a flea market or on the Internet. Many of these authors have been my mentors guiding me through unknown territory: breeding, whelping, handling and training. All have offered knowledge and delight. I hope they give the same to you.

BOOKS

Breed-Specific

With the exception of *The New Complete Pembroke Welsh Corgi,* the books listed here are all older. They give an interesting look at Corgis as a breed 20 or more years ago, while much of the information still holds true for the breed today.

Albin, Dickie. *The Family Welsh Corgi.* London: Popular Dogs Publishing Company Ltd., 1970.

Berndt, Robert J. *Your Welsh Corgi Cardigan—Pembroke.* Fairfax, Virginia: Denlinger, 1978.

Harper, Deborah S. *The New Complete Pembroke Welsh Corgi.* New York: Howell Book House, 1994.

Lister-Kaye, Charles. *The Popular Welsh Corgi.* New York: Arco Publishing Company, 1961.

Perrins, Leslie. *The Welsh Corgi.* London: Wyman and Sons, Ltd., 1958.

Care and Behavior

Bergman, Goran. *Why Does Your Dog Do That?* New York: Howell Book House, 1982.

Coren, Stanley. *The Intelligence of Dogs.* New York: Bantam Books, 1994.

Kirk, Robert W., DVM. *First Aid for Pets.* New York: E.P. Dutton, Inc., 1985.

The Monks of New Skete. *How to Be Your Dog's Best Friend.* Boston: Little, Brown, and Company, 1978.

Rutherford, Clarice, and David H. Neil, MRCVS. *How to Raise a Puppy You Can Live With.* Loveland, Colorado: Alpine Publications, 1981.

Vine, Louis, DVM. *The Total Dog Book.* New York: Warner Books, 1977.

Volhard, Wendy, and Kerry Brown, DVM. *The Holistic Guide for a Healthy Dog.* New York: Howell Book House, 1995.

Training

This is a mixed bag of books, with several different training methods. Not every training method is right for every dog—or every person. Some methods work better than others, even within the same breed. Some of it has to do with the dog; some of it has to do with the person. Study the different methods to find the one you're comfortable with, or build your own method by mixing techniques. If you're just starting out, author Carol Benjamin offers practical advice in easy-to-understand language. Try these titles as well:

Ammen, Amy. *Training in No Time.* New York: Howell Book House, 1995.

Benjamin, Carol Lea. *Dog Problems.* New York: Howell Book House, 1989.

Benjamin, Carol Lea. *Mother Knows Best: The Natural Way to Train Your Dog.* New York: Howell Book House, 1985.

Benjamin, Carol Lea. *Second-Hand Dog.* New York: Howell Book House, 1988.

Benjamin, Carol Lea. *Surviving Your Dog's Adolescence.* New York: Howell Book House, 1993.

Evans, Job Michael. *People, Pooches, and Problems—Understanding, Controlling, and Correcting Problem Behavior in Your Dog.* New York: Howell Book House, 1991.

Evans, Job Michael. *Training and Explaining—How to Be the Dog Trainer You Want to Be.* New York: Howell Book House, 1995.

Haggerty, Capt. Arthur J., and Carol Lea Benjamin. *Dog Tricks—Teaching Your Dog to Be Useful, Fun, and Entertaining.* New York: Howell Book House, 1982.

Koehler, William. *The Koehler Method of Dog Training.* New York: Howell Book House, 1986.

Pearsall, Margaret. *The Pearsall Guide to Successful Dog Training.* New York: Howell Book House, 1982.

Siegal, Mordecai, and Matthew Margolis. *Good Dog, Bad Dog.* New York: New American Library, 1973.

Volhard, Joachim, and Gail Tamases Fisher. *Training Your Dog—The Step-by-Step Manual.* New York: Howell Book House, 1986.

Woodhouse, Barbara. *Dog Training My Way.* New York: Berkley Books, 1983.

Woodhouse, Barbara. *No Bad Dogs: The Woodhouse Way.* New York: Summit Books, 1982.

Showing Your Dog

Craige, Patricia. *Born to Win—Breed to Succeed.* Wilsonville, Oregon: Doral Publishing, 1997.

Hall, Lynn. *Dog Showing for Beginners.* New York: Howell Book House, 1994.

Migliorini, Mario. *Secrets of Show Dog Handling.* New York: Arco Publishing Company, 1982.

Sabella, Frank T. *The Art of Handling Show Dogs.* Hollywood: B and E Publications, 1980.

Breeding

Seranne, Ann. *The Joy of Breeding Your Own Show Dog.* New York: Howell Book House, 1984.

Walkowicz, Chris, and Bonnie Wilcox, DVM. *Successful Dog Breeding—The Complete Handbook of Canine Midwifery.* New York: Arco Publishing, Inc., 1985.

General

American Kennel Club. *The Complete Dog Book.* New York: Howell Book House, 1997.

Lyon, McDowell. *The Dog in Action.* New York: Howell Book House, 1982.

Just for Fun

This part of the list could go on forever. I tried to limit this section to books that feature Corgis only, but a few others just had to be included! Fortunately, you won't have to limit yourself when it comes to wonderful books about dogs . . . even if they aren't Corgis.

Brown, Rita Mae, and Sneaky Pie Brown. *Rest in Pieces, a Mrs. Murphy Mystery.* New York: Bantam Books, 1993. (This series features a cat and a Corgi.)

Carmichael, Emily. *Finding Mr. Right.* New York: Bantam Books, 1999. (A woman returns to life as a Corgi to help her friend.)

Dowell, Karen. *Cooking with Dogs.* Deer Isle, Maine: Two Dog Press, 1998. (This book offers some wonderful poems about dogs, and you don't have to won a specific breed to enjoy it. Poem titles include "Food," "Common Scents," "Animal Hospital" and "English as a Second Language.")

Elias, Esther. *Profile of Glindy.* North Quincy, Massachusetts: The Christopher Publishing House, 1976. (The story of a Pembroke Welsh Corgi imported from Wales and his life with the author. Funny and sad and loving, as are all the true stories of Corgis.)

Elias, Esther. *The Queening of Ceridwen.* West Hanover, Massachusetts: The Christopher Publishing House, 1982. (A continuation of the story begun in *Profile of Glindy.*)

Guillot, Rene. *Little Dog Lost.* New York: Lothrop, Lee and Shepard, 1970. (This book is about a Corgi puppy who gets lost in the forest and is raised by a vixen.)

King, Dorothea. *Rex, Q.C.* Boston: Little, Brown, and Company, 1984. (Life as a Royal, as seen through the eyes of Rex, Queen's Corgi.)

McCaig, Donald. *Eminent Dogs Dangerous Men.* New York: HarperCollins, 1991. (This book is about the author's search through Scotland for a Border Collie. Although it is not about Corgis, it is about a herding breed and is so well written, you won't mind that it's not your chosen breed.)

McCaig, Donald. *Nop's Trials.* New York: Crown, 1984. (A novel about a Border Collie. If you're interested in herding, this can give you some insight, and even if you're not, it's a gripping story.)

Smith, Arthur D. *Shorty.* Grand Rapids, Michigan: AKA Publishers, International, 1985. (Art Smith's illustrations and text combine to create a wonderful story of a boy and his dog.)

Tudor, Tasha. *Corgiville Fair.* New York: Thomas Y. Crowell Company, 1971. (Tasha Tudor's famous artwork creates a wonderful world of rabbits, bogarts [read the book] and Corgis.)

Tudor, Tasha. *The Great Corgiville Kidnapping.* New York: Little, Brown, and Company, 1997. (The Corgiville characters return with a kidnapping adventure.)

VIDEOS

The American Kennel Club Video Series offers videos on a variety of subjects.

Pembroke Welsh Corgi illustrates the Standard.

Dog Steps, from the book of the same name by Rachel Paige Elliot, gives a wonderful study of movement.

A Day in the Life of a Ring Steward is invaluable if you plan to steward. It also helps you understand ring procedure.

For a complete list of the AKC videos, call or write:

The American Kennel Club
5580 Centerview Dr.
Raleigh, NC 27606
919-233-9780

Index